WAR TIME STORIES

An Illinois Soldier's Civil War Experiences

By Daniel O. Root

From the Newman (Illinois) *Independent*

Edited by Richard A. Chrisman

Order this book online at www.trafford.com
or email orders@trafford.com

Most Trafford titles are also available at major online book retailers.

Printed in the United States of America.

ISBN: 978-1-4269-7248-5 (sc)
ISBN: 978-1-4269-7249-2 (e)

Trafford rev. 06/18/2011

 www.trafford.com

North America & international
toll-free: 1 888 232 4444 (USA & Canada)
phone: 250 383 6864 ♦ fax: 812 355 4082

TABLE OF CONTENTS

Preface   vii

Introduction   By Daniel O. Root   xiii

Chapter One   Initiation into War   1

Chapter Two   The Siege and Capture of Corinth   16

Chapter Three   The Bay Springs Expedition   47

Chapter Four   Between Battles   68

Chapter Five   The Battles of Iuka and Corinth   89

Chapter Six   After the Battles   116

Endnotes   131

PREFACE

The material in this book appeared in weekly installments in the Newman *Independent*, Newman, Illinois, from August 1, 1902 through May 1, 1903, and was written by Daniel O. Root, who had served for a period of sixteen months in Company H of the 25th Illinois Volunteer Infantry. While he uses some uncommon words and spelling, the articles are printed as written except for some rearrangement to make the order more chronological, adding section headings, and the correction of some obvious typographical errors; The dates the articles appeared are noted. Daniel served until October of 1862, when he was discharged because of disability; five of his brothers also enlisted in the Union army, one of whom died in service.

In these articles that he called "War Time Stories," Mr. Root who identified himself as R. O. D., recounts his exposure to war and death in his initial assignment to Missouri in the fall of 1861. He recalls his experiences at the siege and capture of Corinth, Mississippi, in the summer of 1862, in an expedition with his unit to Bay Springs as well as the battles for Iuka in Corinth in the fall. A major part of his experiences involved encounters with Confederate citizens, including the release of a slave woman and her child, and the spectacle of slaves streaming into Union lines. He recounts his experience with army discipline, attempts to locate the grave of a friend killed in battle, and an encounter with an armed Conference soldier. He tells about paroling captured enemy soldiers, and philosophizes about what makes soldiers brave and his questions of conscience about what he should have done about a mortally wounded enemy soldier.

These articles purport to be accurate accounts of Mr. Root's experiences; he did not have to depend solely on forty-year old memories, but was able to utilize a diary he had written at the time and a memorandum. He was widely read and made many quotations from the Bible and literature, most of which have been identified.

The 25th Regiment of Illinois Volunteers was recruited in the spring and summer of 1861, and mustered in August 4 in Mattoon. The regiment was composed of companies from Coles, Edgar, Champaign, Vermilion and Iroquois counties, as well as Root's home county of Douglas, with William N. Coler of Champaign in command. His service, from July 27, 1861 to October 13, 1863, would take him to Missouri and Arkansas and south through Kentucky and Tennessee to northern Mississippi, and finally to the army hospital at Mound City, Illinois. He was not always with his unit, being in detached service part of the time.

Mr. Root was born in Decatur Township, Washington County, Ohio, September 24, 1834, the second son and third of twelve children born to Levi and Polly Stewart Root. The family moved to the Hocking River near the village of Stewart in Athens County, where they lived until Daniel left for Ohio Wesleyan University at Delaware, Ohio. During his time at the select school in the neighborhood and at the university he also worked on the farm, in a woolen factory, and as a clerk in his uncle D. B. Stewart's country store.

Because of ill health he left the university at the age of twenty, then moved west to Douglas (then Coles) County, arriving at Brushy Fork, October 17, 1854.

Daniel taught the 1854-55 term at the Catfish Point School, near Isabel in Edgar County, then farmed after his marriage to Mrs. Sarah Winkler, April 5, 1855, until he enlisted in the army. Sarah had inherited the farm from her first husband, Charles V. Winkler. She died October 28, 1881, and their daughter Harriet became her father's housekeeper and the caretaker of the younger children.

After the war Daniel returned to the farm, where he remained until moving to Tuscola in 1873 at the beginning of his political career. When Newman Township was organized in 1868, he was chosen moderator of the first meeting. Four years later he served as Assistant Marshall of the census, then was elected Assessor of Newman Township for four terms, after which he served as County Clerk for nine years. He was considered "an excellent authority in public matters."

In 1884 he went into the retail business, entering into partnership in Newman first with James Gillogly and in 1888 with his brother Lawrence E. His business survived a disastrous fire that destroyed the building in March of 1903.

An active Methodist, he first became a member of the Church in Ohio at the age of 17, in January of 1851. After moving to Illinois, he became a part of the society that met in Hopkins School House on Brushy Fork Creek, transferring to Newman in 1858 when that village was organized and a church begun. He was a charter member of this church and helped haul the lumber for the building. Daniel served as secretary of the building committee when this church was replaced with another in 1900-01, as well as writing and reading an historical sketch of the church at its dedication.

He attended church regularly, served as a Sunday School teacher, and was a member of the Official Board for 33 consecutive years. His familiarity with the Bible is evident in his quotations from it in the articles he wrote.

Active in all moral and religious efforts, he belonged to the Masonic Lodge, Knights Templar, Odd Fellows, and Royal Templars of Temperance. He was elected secretary and historian of the Douglas County Old Settlers in 1907. Daniel maintained an active interest in veterans affairs, attending the reunions and other patriotic activities. When Mr. and Mrs. Scott Burgett gave a social at their home for the veterans of the Civil War and the Spanish-American War in 1903, he gave a talk on "Fallen Heroes of Newman and Vicinity." His eventful life came to a close February 18, 1917.

Many individuals and libraries have assisted in the annotation of the text, including Margaret Rogers, Northeast Mississippi Museum Association, Corinth, Mississippi; Dick D. Grube, National Infantry Museum, Fort Benning, Georgia; Dr. Ben Earl Kitchens, Iuka, Mississippi; Lynnita Sommer, Douglas County Museum, Tuscola, Illinois; Ed Russow, Lincoln Library, Springfield, Illinois; Don Richter, Vermilion County Museum Society, Danville, Illinois; Donna Watson, Archives and Historical Library, the Wesleyan Church, Indianapolis, Indiana; Charlotte Wax, Newman, Illinois; Jane Chamberlin, Illinois Wesleyan University, Bloomington, Illinois; and Dr. Donald E. Sutherland, professor of history at the University of Arkansas, Fayetteville. To each of these I am deeply indebted.

Daniel O. Root

DANIEL O. ROOT'S INTRODUCTION

TO "WAR TIME STORIES"

When in a reminiscent mood, which as age creeps on at decreasing intervals, the scenes and incidents of the long ago pass in review before our mind's eye, in apparently as real form, as when they actually occurred in the days when our mental and physical energies were most active and stronger.

And as one of these moods is now upon the writer, he is tempted, with your permission, Mr. Editor, [1] to relate a few of the many incidents that came under his own observation, and have left their impress upon his mind which the mood aforesaid has revived—while he was wearing the blue during the late "unpleasantness between the States." He dare not hope, nor should the reader expect him, to relate them, as graphically as would one who draws largely upon his own imagination for material. He will promise that the "tales" shall possess one merit at least, that of truth, tho' in a homely garb, perhaps, unless his eyes and ears have deceived him.

[July 11, 1902]

CHAPTER ONE:

INITIATION INTO WAR

The 25ᵗʰ Infantry Sent to Missouri

It will be remembered by those who are familiar with the history of the war that there was gathered an immense army under General John C. Fremont, the intrepid "pathfinder," who "planted upon the top most crag the flag of all the free," as was sung of him in 1856 when he was the first candidate of the republican party for the presidency of the United States; and who ran off with the daughter, Jessie, of "Old Bullion" Benton and was married to her by a Catholic priest, who did not care what he did, as a "stumper" naively put it in answering the charge that Fremont was a Catholic because he had been married by a priest of that church. Under this man let it be repeated was gathered an army of some 30,000 in the fall of 1861, and was encamped in and adjacent to Springfield, Mo. Among the troops composing this army was the 25ᵗʰ Ill. Infy. Co H, of which was recruited in Douglas County, the writer being one of the number, with this great army he had nothing to do as far as its movements are concerned, and he simply mentions the fact of his being gathered at Springfield at this time, as the basis of the incident he is about to relate. That fearful disease—a regular army scourge—broke out in portions of this army in Oct. 1861, and took many a recruit to the land where war is unknown, before they had had an opportunity of meeting the foe. They had left mother and home endearment to measure arms with the enemy, falling on the gory fields, and had left others with health so impaired that they sooner or later were discharged and sent home to die, or linger on as physical wrecks.

When it was decided to withdraw the army encamped around Springfield, to points more accessible to the bases of supplies, it became a serious question how the sick were to be disposed of, as it was at least 125 miles to the nearest railroad points, Rolla and Sedalia, each being distant that far, and they were the nearest points. Arrangements were finally made to send such as were supposed to be able to endure the exposure, to Rolla, and then to St. Louis. The supply of ambulances was not sufficient to accommodate the wants, and road wagons were pressed into service, and prepared for the use intended, to make up the deficiency.

These, with the ambulances, made 150 vehicles, and was in charge of Lieut. Col. J. S. McClelland [2] of the 25th Ill. Reg., who was a physician of note, before entering the service, and withal a man with a heart large enough to take in the world—just the man for such a mission. As two of the writer's messmates—William and Eli Hopkins, brothers of our fellow townsman, Samuel Hopkins and Mrs. Scott Burgett [3] being among the number, he naturally felt an interest in their welfare, and succeeded in getting another of his messmates, the big hearted and whole souled Jerry Ishum, [4] well known to the old timers on Brushy Fork,[5] selected as one of the nurses.

The train loaded with its precious living freight, on the first day was late in starting, and only got cleverly strung out and under way when it went into camp, some five or six miles east of the city. And after the sick and teams had been properly cared for, and the evening meal over, Col. McClelland called his drivers, guards and nurses before him, and delivered himself of a little speech of the following import: "Boys, I have called you together, to say to you that we are now charged with an important, in fact a sacred duty, which is to care for and safely deliver, at Rolla, these unfortunate sick and helpless boys. Now I am myself a physician and know something of the needs and requirements of the sick, and I know that army rations, while good for the well soldier, are very poor substitutes for chicken and its broth for the sick and convalescing. And it is very unfortunate that the army regulations prohibit foraging, except under severe restrictions, which I have not the power to change, or enforce, so you see we are handicapped on this matter. But I want you to see to it that these boys do not suffer for want of proper care and diet."

The Colonel in telling the writer of this incident, upon his return from the trip, said that he really wanted and expected his listeners to read between the lines and keep the chicken supply up to the demand, and they did.

The next evening the caravansary went into camp near a farm house, and the proprietor, a pleasant old gentleman, came to the colonel and said to him in substance and in meekness and truthfulness, seemingly, that he had been despoiled of about all his possessions except his lands and they would have been carried away or eaten on the spot if it had been possible. Both armies, he said, had taken a hand in the spoilation of his substance, until nothing was left him but three stands of bees and he wished the colonel would be

3

so considerate as to place a guard over the remnant of his life's savings, the three bee gums and their contents. And he promised.

At guard mounting a sentinel was placed near the hives that were in danger, but the nature of his instructions and duties, if indeed any were given, could not be traced with any degree of certainty to any source. Daylight the next morning however did develop the fact that a sentinel was standing in his place, but the bee hives were not, and that the owner thereof was terribly "put out," and equally as helpless to restore his loss, and he showed it too. The sentinel when interrogated about the matter, said he had not been told to guard any bees, that in fact there were no bee hives in sight when he took his station, to be guarded.

"What," said the colonel, "were you stationed there to do then?"

"Nothing, sir" was the reply, and the investigation ended. The guard had been kept faithfully up all night, relieved every two hours however, but guarding nothing.

The colonel in reporting the incident remarked with apparent pleasure and many sly winks at his listeners, that judging from the appearance of the mess table that morning, if the milk had been a little better distributed, they had struck a "land flowing with milk and honey." [6] He further stated that someone during the night had invaded his culinary department and for the want of something better to hold it, had filled his coffee pot with the "nectar of ambrosial sweetness fit for the gods."

And by the way the sick and convalescing were not overlooked, for something with a flavor as appetizing as that of the quail in the wilderness was to the wandering tribes of the children of Israel, [7] had been gathered or caught somewhere, picked, cooked and stewed for those now helpless but brave defenders of "Old Glory," the "Rules of War" and the "Army Regulations," to the contrary notwithstanding.

The Death of a Young Soldier

But a sadder scene was in store for this caravan of unfortunates, but one very liable to occur in any army. The roads between Springfield and Rolla, you know, are very mountainous ones, and in 1861 the country through which they passed was very thinly settled and poorly improved. One night this train encamped at the foot of a steep rugged mountain facing the south, and near a small stream of water. During the night a boy in one of the ambulances [8] died suddenly, which cast a gloom over the little camp in the dense forest and mountains and remote from the abode of men. A rude box had been constructed for a coffin and the remains was laid therein as tenderly as could be by his comrades, a grave on the sunny side of the mountain a few rods above the road and overlooking it, was prepared, and just as the sun's first rays struck and lighted up the mountain side and the open grave, the funeral cortege, small in number and in the plain dress of the Union soldiery, slowly and solemnly wended its way up the mountain slope, the rude box containing the remains, borne by sorrowing comrades, the guard of honor with arms reversed closely following, presented a scene that affected even to solemnity, the heart of the grim soldier whose every mission courts death in hideous forms. Arriving at the grave the body was lowered to its last resting place, the honor of war due his rank was paid, and silently with solemn tread the simple funeral party left one of their number, "to sleep the sleep that knows no waking." [9] Far from home and loved ones and alone, but saddest of all, perhaps, is the reflection that this dear soldier boy may have had a loving mother, a devoted sister and a maiden lover, whose hearts were broken over an irreparable loss.

> So never to the desert won [worn?]
>> Did fount bring freshness sweeter,
> Than that he's [his?] placid rest this morn,
>> Has brought this shrouded sleeper.
>
> That rest may tap his weary head,
>> Where channels choke the city,
> Or when mid woodland by his bed
>> The wren shalt make its ditty.
>
> But near or far while evening's star,
>> Is dear to hearts regretting,
> Around that spot admiring thought
>> Shall hover unforgetting. [10]

[March 20, 1903]

It was, the reader will remember, just after the sad burial on the mountain slope in the early morn, of a comrade who had died during the night in an ambulance, with no loving hand of a wife, a mother or a sister to minister to his wants; cheer his passage o'er the Stygian Pool [11] and follow his simple bier and rude coffin to the lonely grave, in the primeval forest on the southern side of a spur of the Ozark mountains. He met the death and had the burial common to a soldier, and peace be to his ashes!

It will be in place here and now to say after the event just noted no incident worth the mention occurred to mar the journey of the caravan or "hospital on wheels" and in good time it arrived at Rolla, and the unfortunate occupants of ambulances and wagons were transferred to railroad coaches and conveyed to hospitals in St. Louis, out of which not a few came in their coffins.

One of these, Wm. Hopkins, was a messmate of the writer; eldest son of the late James Hopkins [12] of this city, a brother of Samuel L. Hopkins and Mrs. Scott Burgett of this city and a young man of more than ordinary intelligence.

The mention of his name brings up an incident in the mind of the writer which he will relate. It occurred soon after we had "donned the blue," and before we learned the best way to hold our muskets, when firing, so as to prevent them from "kicking" us over, or kicking themselves out of our hands and landing a rod or so behind us. Hopkins, or Will, as his messmates called him, had been on guard, and when relieved he, with the rest of the guards, were marched to the bank of the river—the Lamine river in Mo.—near which the 25th Ill. Infy. was then encamped, for the purpose of discharging their pieces before returning to camp; for loaded guns are dangerous things to be "stacked" or loosely lying around the tents.

At this time the regiment was armed with the old Springfield muskets that had once been "flintlocks." Smooth bored, but changed into percussion locks, and were about as dangerous at the breech as at the muzzle. The guards were brought into line along the water's edge and ordered to fire into the bank on the opposite side of the river. When they had come to the proper position the officer of the guards said "Make ready, Take aim, Fire!" And fire they did, but it brought confusion, and as Uncle Billy Shute [13] used to say, "A right smart bit of fun," as well. Some of the muskets acted in very unruly manner. Comrade Hopkins' musket, for instance, "kicked" viciously, raising the breech from the shoulder in less time than you can wink, sending it backward like a flash over his shoulder, landing it several feet in the rear. In its flight the "hammer" on the lock tore off quite a slice of the skin of Will's face, causing the blood to flow very freely, making an ugly wound. As Will came into the company quarters, swinging his old musket in one hand by the strap, and in the other a handkerchief with which he was wiping the claret from his face; the writer met him and seeing his plight, which alarmed him, he added excitedly: "What's the matter Will?" And he, without checking his pace, but with faint attempt at a smile, replied: "Ask the old musket."

The fact was that these old time army muskets could "Kick" worse than any army mule, and the majority of new recruits—and the entire regiment was then in that class—feared the "butt" of their own guns as much as they did the muzzle of the enemy's. The writer is quite certain that he did not discharge his own musket loaded with a full charge for three months after he began to drill in the "manual of arms" for fear of the "butt end" consequences. He would withdraw his load; on the sly, and fire a blank shot, to keep up the appearance of bravery. The old "kicker" could, it is true, send an ounce ball 5,280 feet, and do execution, too, if it found anything to do it on; but it was very uncertain as to the course it did not always go as the birds fly—in a straight line. It may be truly said, the writer believes, that any soldier, who for a period of ninety days, manipulated one of these guns, and received its oft repeated "kicks" certainly is entitled to a pension without an additional cause being assigned or required. Of course the writer forfeited his chances under this head of securing a grip upon Uncle Sam's money boxes, by using blank cartridges when he was required to "fire off" his musket. But he missed many a bruise, and escaped hours of anxiety and dread which is some compensation you know.

Pride Goes Before a Fall

Now let the writer tell another on himself, illustrating what foolish things even an otherwise intelligent soldier may do under certain conditions. He rather prided himself on the skill and accuracy with which he could manipulate his musket, according to harder tactics from "Shoulder arms" to take aim and fire. And it was in an endeavor to indicate and defend his expertness and knowledge that he was "caught napping" and thus humiliated. He was on guard—camp guard—the purpose of which was more to keep the blue coats inside than it was to keep the gray coats out. His beat was a long one, in an open field and some distance from camp. While leisurely pacing his, at about the middle of the forenoon, a solider from the camp came up and attempted to cross the guard line without recognizing the sentinel; but the sentinel halted him, and at the same time bringing the "arms" into the position enjoined by the "manual of arms." The corporal, for that was the rank of the intruder, stopped at the command to halt, but said in reply, you did not bring your gun into the proper position to halt one, the guard indicated that he had, while the corporal contended he had not, and at the same time, the corporal was advancing toward the sentinel. The contention at length waxed hot, the guard getting hot under the collar, and the corporal was getting, apparently, in a like frame of mind. But it was only apparently so, not real, for he was "on to his job" and in due time, when the guard was fully on his grounds the corporal said in a persuasive tone, "Hand me your gun and I will show you how it is done." And he got it, too, strange as it may seem that a soldier on guard would so far forget himself as to give up his "arms" merely for the asking. Now said the corporal, "I'll go and report you." And while he did not do so, and perhaps never intended to do so, yet he could have

Daniel O. Root

done it and had a good cause, too, which might in the end, have sent the writer's boasted knowledge of the "manual of arms" and other soldierly qualities "glimmering."

This corporal, was Daniel Jacobs, [14] well known to the war time citizens of Newman, and now a resident of Nebraska. He was a member of the writer's company and a brave soldier.

[May 1, 1903]

The 25th Regiment Transferred to Tennessee

By the early part of May, 1862, the 25th Ill. Reg.—to which the writer belonged—was transferred from the army of the Southwest, to the army of the Tenn. At the time the transfer was made the regiment was in camp at Batesville, Ark., on White river, in Gen. Curtis' Division. The transfer was a fortunate affair, for had it not taken place, the regiment would have been in the disastrous Red river campaign under Curtis and Banks.

The distance from Batesville to Cape Girardeau on the Mississippi river, between St. Louis and Cairo, is about two hundred and fifty miles and made by the troops transferred by forced marches, in the ten days, an average of twenty-five miles a day, ten or twelve miles being considered a "day's march." We marched five days and "laid off" one day for rest, and a clean up, and then set in again, reaching the cape at the eleventh day from the start. The regiment camped outside the town, but the writer was permitted to go into it, and he spent the night with a "mess" of neighbor boys in Co. D of the 21st Ill. Inf. which was also one of the transferred regiments, and encamped in the town. A storm, with wind, thunder and lightning, came up during the night that was frightful and destructive as well; demolishing tents, and unroofing buildings. The tent of the Fremont pattern, containing the Newman "mess" and its visitor, escaped demition, but they got wet up a little, the wind driving the rain right through the heavy tent cloth.

Every morning of the last three days' march some portions of our camp equipage was burned to lighten our transportation, as our teams were giving out. It was burned to prevent it from falling into the hands of the enemy.

There were ten regiments in all detached from the army of the South-west, and sent to reinforce the army of the Mississippi, then besieging Corinth. Among those regiments were the 21st, 25th, 35th, 36th, 44th, and 59th Ill., the 8th, 18th, and 22nd Ind., and all were camped in and around Batesville and Pocahontas, Ark., at the time the order for their transfer was made, and it was said that there was a rivalry sprung up between the brigade commanders as to which command should reach the Mississippi river first—hence the race or forced march, described above.

The writer was fortunate in having a horse to ride on this march, he being at the time his Colonel's orderly, but he is glad to say that he let several of his less fortunate comrades share with him in the riches.

A Shameless Crime and its Punishment

An incident, vile and shameful, one that brought the blush of mortification to the cheek of every honest soldier, occurred on this march and while it is of such a character that it cannot be given in detail, yet, in order to show the manner in which such revolting crimes were dealt with in the army, and in an emergency, the writer will merely state its nature, leaving the details for the imagination to work out, and give in more detail the mode of punishment inflicted upon the perpetrators.

One night some three days after the march began, two men, members of the 22nd Ind. Gen. Jeff C. Davis' old regiment, stole out of camp and went to a farm house not far distant and informed the occupants—two women, [mother] and daughter, the former 80 years old, and both widows, that they had been sent to guard their premises. To this they of course could urge no objections, and the daughter to accommodate the supposed friendly and honest guards, made a pallet on the floor for them, there being no spare bed in the house. But immediately upon the completion of the temporized bed, one of the self styled guards assaulted her, committing a nameless crime, which was repeated by the other guard, while the first committed a like crime upon the old lady who had retired for the night.

They then returned to camp, followed by the younger woman, as soon as she had recovered from the shock sufficiently to enable her to do so. Her story aroused the officers of the regiment to which the guilty soldiers belonged, to immediate and determined action, and they were soon run down and fully identified by the woman, and placed under guard; had her evidence taken in full.

The importance of reaching the Mississippi river, at the earliest possible moment prevented further proceedings at that time, for it was then time the army should be on the road. But that night after a long, weary march, Gen. Davis convened a "Drum Head" court martial to try the case of the two desperadoes, under guard. Of this court Lieut. Col. McClelland of the 25th Reg. and then in command of it, was a member and as the writer was his orderly and "bunked" with him he got his information relating to the court proceedings from first hands, and knew the result in advance of their publication to the army. The details however need not be given here, and for the same reason that the details of the heinous assault were not given. It may suffice it to say that the court found them guilty as charged, and they were sentenced to have their polls shaven clean, the leader's with a razor, and the other's with shears, and then "drummed" out of camp and the union lines.

Gen. Davis remarked when examining the findings of the emergency court that if he had been certain it would not have been establishing a precedent, for the punishment of such crimes in the army, he would have favored the shooting of the men on the spot, and the writer is more than half persuaded that is what should have been done.

Their punishment, however, was severe and most humiliating to anyone not entirely bereft of consciousness [conscience?] , and void of every principle of manhood. It is presumable in this case however, that the perpetrators of this grave crime, were bereft of one and devoid of the other, of these virtues and that the army and world would have suffered no loss by their going out of both, at one and the same time and that, too, by the shortest and quickest route—gunpowder and lead—for "electrocution" was not then practiced on state or army criminals.

The next morning, shortly after the army had got in motion, and a suitable place in the road had been reached, it was halted and brought to "open order" the sentence of the court martial was duly executed. During the night the prisoners had been prepared strictly to orders. The head of the leader in the assault was a horrible sight, of ghastly whiteness, smooth and glossy as the finest varnish, in the hands of an expert could make it, which glistened in the sunlight like a gilded dome, added to which was the erratic motion given to it by the movement of the body in walking that intensified the hobgoblin appearance of the wretch. The other desperado was very little less horrible in appearance. His head lacked somewhat in whiteness and gilding, but otherwise they matched well, and either of them would adorn a "Rogue's March" and never be mistaken for gentlemen.

The line of the army extended a mile or more perhaps, and were at "open order" and "facing inward." The "drumming out" outfit, beside the two outlaws consisted of two regimental field bands, and six guards. They started playing the "Rogues' March," the two worse than rogues next, and at their heels the guards with "fixed bayonets" pointed at the fleshiest part of the two who were furnishing the principal attraction of the occasion, whose heads were hatless as well as hairless.

[November 21, 1902]

The procession, in many respects amusing and eliciting various remarks from the men in the ranks, not in any manner complimentary to the malefactors, who never turned their shorn heads to the right or left, but kept their eyes cast upon the ground, showing no signs of hearing or heeding the illy suppressed jeerings of the boys in the line.

The procession passed through the entire length of the open ranks, then "about face" and returned in the same order to the place of beginning, thence on and out into a dense forest among the spurs and vales of the Ozark mountains where the despised and dishonored twain were left to their fate, to ponder and reflect upon the enormity of their crime and realize fully that the "way of the transgressor is hard."[15] What became of either of them the writer never knew. A vague rumor said that one of them turned up in Cairo, Ill., and again entered the army, some ten months after his "drumout," as herein noted. It is more reasonable to suppose that he and his mate as well, run shy of the union army during the continuance of the war at least. It would have been a redeeming act if they had have suicided in the cleft of some massive rock in the wilds of the Ozark regions, where none but cayots [coyotes] and vultures could look upon their carcasses.

[November 28, 1902]

CHAPTER TWO

THE SIEGE AND CAPTURE OF CORINTH, MISSISSIPPI

Transported to the Scene of Action

In his last communication the writer left his regiment at Cape Girardeau, on its way to join the forces investing Corinth. [16] He attempted to detail briefly the march from Batesville to the Cape and the disgraceful incident that occurred on the march. He will now endeavor to relate the incidents briefly that came under his notice on the trip by steamer, from Cape Girardeau to Hamburg on the Tennessee river and in the vicinity of the Shiloh battlefield, and the part taken by his regiment in the siege of Corinth, culminating in its evacuation by the Confederates May 30, 1862. Gen. Davis' Division got into the Cape on the evening of May 20th and left for Corinth as soon and as fast as transports could be obtained. The writer's regiment got off on the evening of the 22nd. Let him here quote from the entry made in his diary that day. "We received orders this morning to move all our traps and regimental belongings into the steamer 'Henry Clay' which was accomplished by 10 o'clock a.m. At 11 o'clock the men were marched aboard and then the horses were put on and at 5 p.m. amid shouts of joy, colors flying, bands playing and hats waving, we steamed out into the father of waters and went dashing down the turbid stream toward Cairo, where we landed at 10 o'clock that evening and remained till morning. During the night one of our men fell overboard and was drowned." [17] The "Henry Clay" was a large old time steamer, that without crowding easily accommodated the 800 men of the regiment, the horses, save 25 perhaps, and the tents and other camp equipage. The boat was in the government service, and was afterward sunk in attempting to run the blockade of Vicksburg, Miss. We cut cable early in the morning and started up the "La Belle" Ohio, plowing through its placid waters like a thing of life, the delighted blue coats enjoying to the full the sight again of the grand old "prairie state," in God's country, after tramping for nine months the rocks, hills and barren wastes of Arkansas and Missouri and hearing the natives [we] meet talking about "we'uns," "yu'ins" and our "niggers." Let the writer again draw upon the notes made in his diary of that date—Friday, May 23*** "Got the mouth of the Tennessee, about 12 a.m.; did not stop at Paducah, but turned without halting into the Tennessee and plodded slowly up the river to within a few miles of the late Fort Henry, and landed and remained over night, fastening the boat to a large tree on the bank of the river. We were paid off to-day, the first time in months. I (the writer) receiving $64.80, four months pay. Our boat has, like the great majority of river crafts, a 'bar' over which liquors flow in endless streams and now that the boys are flush, there will no doubt, be boisterous times aboard, with the free spending of money that should be sent to destitute families at home. 'Tis passing strange that the government will permit wide open 'bars' to be run on boats in its own exclusive service. Many of the boys went on shore, cooked their rations and slept on the ground."

At early morn the old craft steamed up and pulled out from shore and began its slow plodding against the strong current and soon the sad effects of the war began to appear. Here were the huge abutments of a railroad bridge hanging at an angle of 45 degrees over the water, the other parts having gone up in smoke and down (the river) in ashes, and there is where Fort Henry stood and not far away Fort Heiman, both confederate strong-holds at the time of their capture February 6, 1862. They were defended by some 3,000 men, under Gen. Tilghman. The fall of Fort Henry led Gen. Grant to the immediate attack upon Fort Donelson, but a few miles away, but on the Cumberland river, which soon surrendered, with 15,000 men under the command of Gen. Buckner, Gen. Floyd and Pillow having fled before the capture. The victories forced Grant to the front and demonstrated that this man of "silence" was to be a man of destiny as well.

Referring again to an entry made at the time in his diary—May 25th, which was Sunday, the writer will quote: "We have quite a treat today. The entire regiment was invited by the Colonel to the 'hurricane deck' which invitation was pretty generally accepted by the boys, who were pleased with the privilege of spending a time on the roof of the boat, where a splendid view of the country could be obtained, when they had gathered together, they were called to order, and informed they had been called up there to have a social meeting and some speech making thrown in, and after a time Maj. McKibben—U. S. Paymaster [18] —who had four sons in Co. H of the 25th Ill. [19] and all present at the time, was called on for a speech and graciously responded, saying in a humorous spirit and tone, among other loyal utterances, that he was proud of them, and they are all in the Union army, and members of this command, and were all present, and boys the only thing I have to regret is, that I did not know forty years ago that this was coming for I could as well have had as many more, which sentiment was uproariously cheered."

Col. Coler, father of "Bird" Coler, [20] who is such a potent element in New York city and state politics and was the democratic candidate for governor at the last election, and who was then present but was too young for the service, our own Col. Taggert, [21] then a captain, of Tuscola, Maj. Nodin [22] and several others also made short addresses. The last named got a little confused in thought and utterances, stammered, see-sawed, spit and then, after succeeding in getting his thoughts and vocal organs in unison sufficiently to enable him to say, with a few cuss words thrown in, that he knew there were privates in the crowd who could make better speeches than he or any officer present could, he subsided. But as he did so he called up by name one of the boys, who arose and responded in a neat little speech that in sense and sentiment was equal to any that had been uttered.

Our boat proved to be a slow coach. Other vessels loaded with transferred troops that had left Cape Girardeau the next day after the "Henry Clay" were now passing us and reached their destination in advance of us. But our boat finally got here, pulling into shore about midway between Pittsburg Landing and Hamburg on the morning of May 26, having run all night. We had been from the evening of the 22nd in making the trip, which an up-to-date boat would have made in much less time.

The regiment disembarked and marched up to Hamburg, only a short distance, and went into camp just south of the village. And during the day we received our uniform clothing of caps, blue frock coats, blue pants, and shoes. Here is all excitement and hustle. Fresh troops coming in hourly, by water and land, and hurrying up to the front, only a few miles to the south. The 25th regiment will move out tomorrow, and in the next installment the writer will endeavor to show the part he and his regiment took in the siege and fall of Corinth.

[November 28.1902]

In his last installment of army reminiscences, he left his regiment in camp in the near vicinity of Hamburg, Miss., they having just arrived by steamer from Cape Girardeau, Mo. In this communication, he also promised to tell the part he and his regiment had taken in the siege of Corinth which was an important strategic point easy of access, being at the cross of the Mobile and Ohio, and the Memphis and Charleston railways and only a few miles from the Tennessee river hence it was a prize worth fighting for, and Uncle Sam was reaching for it without stint.

The confederates under Gen. Beauregard were defending the place with 53,000 men, while the Federals, numbering 100,000 perhaps under Halleck and Pope were daily tightening their grip upon the doomed town, which proved to be not so strongly defended as it was supposed to be by the Federals before its evacuation.

Horseplay Leads to Unfortunate Consequences

The 25th moved to the front the day following its arrival at Hamburg, and went into camp near Farmington, and only some 3½ miles from Corinth. The road was over ridges and through swamps, that part of it from the river to the bluffs two miles or more in length, was made of logs and poles, the logs at the bottom and the poles at the top, raising the road some four or five feet above the surface of the ground, and was rough enough to jolt the daylights out of a jumping jack, if it should attempt to pass over it in any sort of a vehicle. The boys called it a "high grade corduroy road;" but it kept one out of the mud and water, which was some compensation for the other bad qualities. The writer well remembers what a time he and Chaplain Phillip N. Mericar [Minear?] [23] had in getting Lieut. Col. McClelland of their regiment over this same corduroy highway one time, shortly after this march. And the writer will digress long enough to briefly relate this incident and its cause. Col. McClelland was a "tall slim and slender" man; six feet two, in his socks, and weighed at his best scarce 120 pounds; in fact he was nigh unto a veritable "walking skeleton," but game to the core.

Captain Lines L. Parker, [24] then a Lieut., once Douglas county's "baby" treasurer, now living at Hugo this county and well known to a majority of the INDEPENDENT'S readers, was, physically, the very reverse of the colonel, weighing then some 250 pounds, not as much as he has since, raised the beam by 150 pounds, not as much as he now lifts it, by nearly as many pounds. Well one day the Capt. was standing in his company's parade grounds when the Col. came up and spoke to him and after a little friendly sparring and bantering between them the Colonel threw his arm around Parker who was standing with his hands in his pockets, and in this maneuvering and frisking around his feet became in some way entangled with a stick or small pole, stumbled and in falling pulled the Capt. over with him, he—the Captain—falling upon the Col. with such force as to break or tear loose several of his ribs, rendering him to all intents and purposes hors-de-combat.[25] Upon an examination of his case by several medical experts, among them the medical director of Gen. Davis' division, it was decided to send him north for treatment, and he having a brother residing in Louisville, Ky., who was a physician, he chose to go there rather than to his home at Indianola, Ill.

The Chaplain of the regiment and the writer were selected to accompany him to the river, and get him aboard of a steamer. He was placed in an ambulance and made as comfortable as circumstances would permit and started for Hamburg, the writer driving, the chaplain mounted on his charger following. Our progress was slow, for the colonel's wound was rather serious and very painful, causing us to make frequent halts, in order to change his position and give him rest. But our real trouble came when we struck the corduroy road, elsewhere mentioned herein, for we had gone not exceeding a half dozen lengths of the ambulance over the bare poles, when the colonel fairly screamed to the driver, to stop, throwing a few cuss words in, to emphasize the force of his yell. It took some time to quiet him for he was greatly excited and suffering intense pain. Finally we got his consent to move on, but the shaking up given to the ambulance by the wheels passing over the poles was too much for the pain it produced and his patience, and he again, with more vigor and emphasis than before ordered a halt. He was in a perfect furor of anger, and oaths, outswearing "our army in Flanders," [26] and said he would get out of this d----- thing," meaning the ambulance, "if it killed him," and we had to take him out too. But fortunately it was not much trouble to do it, for he did not weigh much more than an ordinary fence rail, and by the way he was nearly as long as one, too, and it was this fact only that caused any trouble handling him. We had to lift him from the ambulance and place him on the corduroy road and from this to the ground some several feet, for he would not lie on the "d----- poles" he said. After spending an half hour or more in the rig, we succeeded this time in getting to the river with him without having to unload him again tho' we had many stops to make in order to stop his screaming and swearing.

A steamer, bound down the river was anchored at the Hamburg wharf, so we transferred the colonel from ambulance to boat, and in due time he reached Louisville and was joined there by his wife, who with his brother—a doctor—nursed him into something like his former self in about ninety days, when he rejoined his regiment.

As before stated, the 25th reg. (and Davis' Division as well) moved out from the river and went into camp in the vicinity of Farmington, and not far from our advance lines. Farmington was a small village, a mere hamlet in fact, was occupied by our forces under Gen. Pope, May 20th, 1862, only a few days before our arrival, after two pretty severe engagements on the 3rd and 9th of May in which the rebels were defeated.

The Lengthy Siege of Corinth

It will be remembered by those familiar with the details of the war, that the siege of Corinth lasted from twelve or fifteen days, and prosecuted with skill and dispatch, [27] (the advance being made by "Parallels," that is by making trenches or ditches for protection and defense, running in parallel lines with each other, our besieging lines were in the shape of a semicircle, or a horseshoe the enemy being within the circle, and Corinth the objective point. Skirmishing between the two armies was daily occurring, somewhere along our advance lines and as we drove the enemy back, we would secure the ground gained by digging new trenches in front of the old ones. These advances would contract our lines and the ditches would strengthen them, by protecting our boys and batteries from the attempts of the enemy to dislodge and drive us back, and in this manner were our forces gradually squeezing the life out of that portion of the confederacy represented by its besieged army in and around Corinth, Miss. In the last days of May, 1862, when Gen. Davis' Division of which the 25th Ill. was a part, came to assist Uncle Sam in the squeezing out process, which was consummated in a very few days thereafter without any serious or destructive battle occurring. But the part the writer and his regiment took in bringing about the happy results of this siege, which he promised in his last installment, to give in his next, must be deferred again until the next, for he has now spun this one out as long as there will be space to contain it, but he will say here and now that he and the old 25th both took part in the "squeeze out" and held a good hand too, and were in the "trenches" on duty, ready to fight or fire as circumstances might determine, all of which certainly will appear in the next communication for he is right now at the point of entering upon the pleasing task of reciting this important event.

[December 5, 1902]

The writer will now endeavor to redeem the promise, at least twice uttered, to give an account of the part taken by his regiment (including himself) in the important siege of Corinth in the latter half of May, 1862. As a starter let him here quote verbatim from an entry made in his diary on May 27th, the day his regiment reached the front and went into camp near Farmington. "We are in one and one-half miles of Farmington—are in Pope's division, on the extreme left of Halleck's lines, are within 3 ½ miles of Corinth. 'I (the writer) don't like the looks of this portion of Miss. It strikes me that it will prove to be very unhealthy for the Northern boys. Prospect for a fight very good. Skirmishing going on daily—from our camp we can hear the constant roar of the cannon. Our boys seem eager for the fray. The nearer I approach the less I seem to fear it, and I think I can 'face the music.'"

Reading this excerpt from his memorandum, forty years after it was written, the writer will readily concede that his language in some particulars is open to criticism. For instance Pope was not in command of a division as we understand that term now, or as it was then understood, by anyone familiar with military terms. Pope then commanded the "left wing" of Halleck's army, and Davis' division was in that part or wing, of it. The writer was not familiar with the terms into which the army investing Corinth was divided, nor the relations that Gens. Nelson, Crittenden, Stanley, Sherman and others sustained to these divisions, for he had not been connected with this army twenty-four hours, at the time the entry was made. The other portions of the quotations will stand against criticism, in the judgment of the writer, notwithstanding the seeming boast of personal valor or bravery on the part of the writer. It would, you know, be a little hard to prove that such were not his feelings at the time, unless the proof came through his own lips which he will now say will not so come. But he admits that the hero to-day may be in the van of the retreat tomorrow.

The Final Assault on Corinth

Recourse will again be had on the writer's notes made in the exciting hours just preceding the fall of Corinth and the hasty retreat of its boasted defenders, notwithstanding they sometimes contain a little "camp news" from a "grape vine" telegram, which every old soldier knows should be taken with many grains of allowance. These notes were taken on the grounds in the book in which they were first written.

"Wednesday, May 28, 1862. About 7 a.m. order came for us to move on to the 'lines' immediately, with two days' rations in haversack and 100 rounds of ammunition to the man, as soon as possible—10 o'clock—we are on our way, the boys apparently in fine spirit. After getting to the front, we were assigned a position on our extreme left to support a battery, but were not called into action during the day. Long before we took our position the ball opened, our pickets were driven in early in the morning, and much fighting was done during the day. I learn we relieved the rebels of seven guns (cannons) and 75 men. As I—the writer was the colonel's orderly, I have a good deal of riding to do, and not much else. I went back and forth from field to camp several times during the day."

On one of these in going from the frontline to the camp his road for some distance ran parallel with our outer works and skirmish lines, and at one place as he passed there was a skirmish going on, that in the end attained the character of a fierce little battle and was in plain view from the road. So the writer sat on his horse and watched the movements of the contending forces with awe and interest, for many minutes. The road was on a ridge overlooking the skirmishers, who were in the edge of some woodland, between which and the road there was quite an ascent, and was bare of timber, leaving an unobstructed view. The firing was so intense at times that the smoke would form into dense clouds over the heads of the respective combatants, cutting off the view entirely for a time. The distance from the writer's view point to the contestants was less than one half mile. So the movements of the men, especially our own men, could readily be seen whenever the smoke would lift, and they reminded one very much of a hive of bees when disturbed or agitated. The writer will never forget this battle scene. It made an impression upon him that time cannot efface. He viewed it calmly, was not excited, for he was not in any danger, so his imagination was not distorted through fear or undue excitement. On his return from camp, after attending to matters calling him there, as he passed the point where the skirmish had taken place, the dead and wounded were being carried off the field, and the men engaged in the hot little affray, were also coming in with depleted ranks. [28] Two of these regiments were the 8th Wis. Infy. and 5th Minn. Infy. and they were encamped on the road near the skirmish line. It will be remembered that "Old Abe" the eagle of historic fame, belonged to the 8th Wis. Well "Old Abe" was in this engagement and the writer had the pleasure of seeing him, sitting on his perch at the top of the regimental flag staff in the hands of the color bearer, coming in with the boys, seemingly as conscious of having done his duty as any of the battle stained men had. Once or twice he spread his wings and raised himself a few feet above his perch, and then gracefully dropped down again to his accustomed seat. This is the only time the writer ever saw this bird, and judging from what he then saw of him he is prepared to take with some degree of credibility many of the stories told of the intelligence and sagacity, manifested by this national bird, after peace and union was restored and "Old Abe" with the rest of the blue coats had donned the garb and assumed the habits of peaceful citizens, he was the drawing card of numerous social religious and political gatherings. And ever after "life's fitful dreams were o'er"[29] with him, his mortal remains—the only kind he had probably—became and is yet, no doubt, the same kind of a card, in some museum of relics and curiosities, where it is safe to leave him, or rather his remains. [30]

Daniel O. Root

On Thursday May 29, the writer's notes state that "early this morning our pickets came in contact with the enemy and a brisk fight resulting, our boys finally falling back as the rebs were entrenched and numbered two to our one."[31] A Mo. and Minn. regiment suffered the brunt of the engagement, skirmishing, going on nearly the entire day. Our regiment remained in trenches until nightfall, when it was relieved by the 35th Ill.

The left wing of the 25th is ordered on picket at 6 in the morning, and the entry for the next day runs as follows: "Friday, May 30, at 6 a.m.; left wing of the regiment went to the outposts as ordered last evening, followed shortly thereafter by the other wing, and just as the different companies had been assigned to their stations, orders come for the regiment to go at once in pursuit of the fleeing rebels, had evacuated Corinth and had gone it was supposed toward Grand Junction, some 18 or 20 miles to the east." This news caused great excitement—drums beating, bugles blowing—aides and orderlies running hither and thither—artillery and wagons rattling—infantry quick stepping—then cheering and hats waving, made music strange and discordant, but by no means unpleasant to loyal hearts. The old 25th, the best of regiments, was soon in marching trim and all joyous and lively she moved off toward the fleeing enemy that she had helped to "squeeze out" of his supposed invulnerable entrenchments, and now having got the rebels on the run, the writer will take them up to his next installment and show that the rebs are better runners than fighters by showing that they out ran us, while we out fought them.

[December 12, 1902]

"Old Abe"

The Confederates Abandon and Federals Occupy Corinth

In his last communication the writer left the rebels on the run and his regiment in pursuit, and proposes in this one to give some of the details of the chase. But first it might not be out of place to mention some of the particulars of their hasty and unexpected retreat. Corinth was supposed to have been protected by strongly constructed forts and outworks, manned by the chivalry of the South, under able commanders, the besieged army had shown no sign of weakness in its defenses anywhere, or lack of men and munitions of war. Their forces at the front seemed to be ample, active and alert. But when our forces in separate detachments under Sheridan, Sherman, Stanley, Hatch, Paine and others, got on their flanks and in their rear, Sherman getting close to their works, they got alarmed and began to get their plunder out of the town, before their works were put to the test. But while they were doing this, they kept a strong force at the front, contesting every foot of the ground as a blind of course to deceive us. Another little event tended also to hasten their retreat. The day that they commenced the removal of army supplies on the night of the 28th, a few shells were thrown by our artillery, fell in such places, in the town, as to cause the enemy to believe that the "Yanks" had got range on the town, and its defenses, when the fact was they were fired at random. It was said that one of these shells struck an engine standing on the track, and disabled it. One dropped near a regiment drawn up in line, and exploded killing some and wounding others, and another landed in a different part of the doomed place, just as if it had been sent there on purpose. So the "Johnnies" had plenty good reasons for believing that the "Feds" knew just where to let these messengers of death drop to do the most good for the senders, and the most harm to the receivers. They made 'em git any way.

Here follows in his notes a number of rumors, some of them wild and windy, so much so, that the writer would fairly blush to reproduce them here. We entered Corinth today for the first time. But we were not the first regiment to enter the town after its evacuation, tho' we might claim the honor of doing so, with as much truth, perhaps, as some others have done. The writer understood at the time, that the 36th Ill. Infy. had that honor, but Comrade J. W. Cook, of this city, claims that portions of his regiment—the 39th Ohio to which he belonged (and he was there too)—were the first to enter the deserted town, and the writer has no inclination to controvert his claim, as he had a brother [32] in Cook's regiment and he does not claim for his own that distinction. So Cook and the 36th Infy fight it out.[33] Upon entering the deserted village, there were evidences on every hand of the haste and disorder in which the enemy must have left. Piles and piles of wagons and harness partly burned were seen, while all sorts of camp equipage that could not be moved shared the same fate, as did also hundreds and hundreds of barrels of pork and beef. Even their dead were left unburied. The writer saw a number of bodies in different places in the outskirts of the town, in various stages of decomposition, and they did not seem to have died from wounds, but from disease. It is the opinion of the writer that these bodies were lying dead in tents used as hospitals, and when these tents were taken down for removal or destruction, and in the confusion and panicky condition of the soldiers and their eagerness to get away the dead were simply left unburied for lack of time. This scene, in fact these scenes, emphasize with force the words of old "grizzly" W. T. Sherman, that "war is hell." [34]

What the enemy could not carry away or destroy fell into our hands. One thing is very certain and that is the loss to the confederacy—leaving out of the consideration the loss of Corinth as a strategic point, which of itself can hardly be estimated--in supplies and munitions of war is very great and when we add to them, the loss of prestige, by their failure to hold the vantage grounds, bringing about a state of demoralization in their army which leads to loss of confidence in their officers and on the rank and file as well. But enough of "episodin'" as Josiah Allen's wife would say. [35]

[December 19, 1902]

Chasing Fleeing Rebels

Now for the chase after the absconding enemy, as promised. The writer believes he can do a better job, one at least based upon facts as he understood them, when he went tramp, tramp, tramping after the limber legged and fleeing enemy, by again calling into requisition his "field notes" made on the tramp, which say for Saturday, May 31st: "Reveille at daybreak—a hasty breakfast; Reg. formed into line, and moved off; went only a short distance and was halted. Remaining on the grounds until nightfall when we marched back a little way, and encamped. The delay was caused by the burning of both the public and railroad bridges spanning the Tuscumbia river, in our front by the enemy who also planted batteries on the opposite side of the river to dispute our passage. We must drive them away before even a temporary bridge can be constructed. Much skirmishing going on many stragglers are being picked up by our cavalry.

"On the 2nd day of June, Davis' Division received orders to march southward on the Okolona road, and as soon as possible the 25th was ready for the road, and moved off with the rest of the division, our road ran over hills and thro' swamps, the country being in every respect uninviting and sparsely settled. If it were not for the principle involved in the war it would not be worth fighting for. Good water was scarce. The wells are deep and are usually bored or drilled, and are eight to ten inches in diameter, the water being drawn by rope and windlass, and long tubular buckets, fitting the well exactly, with a valve in the bottom, which the weight of the bucket when it reaches the water forces open, and as it settles into water fills, and when raised out of the water, the water inside the bucket closes the valve and holds intact the contents. These wells may answer for house purposes in a small family perhaps, but would be poor excuses on a stock farm in the wild and wooly west no doubt.

An amusing incident occurred one day between Sergeant Watson, [36] a comrade of the writer's, and a "missus" of the house and plantation at one of these wells, which the writer will relate as it illustrates the intelligence, of at least one Southern lady, and—the rattle of her tongue as well. It happened on one of our marches after retreating rebels, the roads being dry and dusty, and the throats of the boys in like condition, and no water in sight to relieve them. In passing a house, one more pretentious than many others on the march, Watson sighted near the house the curb and other paraphernalia of an old fashioned country well, and breaking ranks, he broke for the well on "the quick step," followed pretty closely by several others, including the writer. Arriving at the well, which was of the kind just attempted to be described, he asked a woman sitting on the porch nearby, who proved to be the "lady" of the house, for permission to slake his thirst. But he had come up against a regular Southern Cyclone, not in the well but in the person of the "missus" who let loose her pent up fury in streams or waves, more forceful than elegant, by far, she called him all the names in the Southern vocabulary that had ever been applied by the chivalry of the South to Northern men, from "mudsills" to "Lincoln hirelings." [37]   She said to him "you are not wanted here," that "you had better be at home minding your own business." This last taunt was the stereotyped phrase in use by all classes of the disloyal, as a supposed clincher. After exhausting her fund of epithets, and herself as well she subsided.

The sergeant then by way of reply and vindication, asked her who began the war by firing the first shot at Fort Sumter, she seemed a little bluffed, but finally said by way of reply, "I declare, I think our people made a mistake, did a great wrong to our cause, in fact, in this matter, for they ought to have killed Mr. Supter when they took him and been done with him." [38]

Remember this wasn't the language of the "poor white trash," but of what was called the "blue blood" of Dixie's land. Comments are not necessary here, further than to say that this woman did not represent the intelligence of the women of the better class of citizens of the South, perhaps, but she was a fair exponent of their unalloyed hatred for Northern men, especially if they wore the blue. Well we haven't caught up with the Johnnies yet, and we may not until they stop for us.

[December 19, 1902]

It will be remembered by the readers, if any there be, of these reminiscent sketches of the war times of 1861-65, that in his last article Gen. Davis' Division in the pursuit of the confederates retreating from Corinth had been turned

South on the Okolona road and was on the tramp, over ridges of yellow clay and sand, and through swamps of black water and boggy soil, with no well defined knowledge, apparently, of the direction the enemy had taken.

Well, resuming where the thread was broken, which was on the morning of June 2nd, 1862. About 11 o'clock a.m., we crossed the Tuscumbia river, on an improvised bridge, near which place the enemy had a few days before masked a battery, against which the 7th Ill. Cavalry ran, and was roughly handled, several being killed, and quite a good many wounded. This battery was silenced, and a temporary bridge put up over which we passed and went on our way rejoicing.

On either side of the road for quite a distance, after crossing the river, large trees had been fallen across the road, completely blocking it, until removed. This was done to delay our advance and give the enemy time to get away with their plunder. From this point the writer was sent back to camp with orders of some character he cannot now recall, and did not return to the front until quite late at night, and he well remembers that in passing through the swamps, and heavy timber on his return trip, he imagined that behind every stump and hill there lurked a "Johnny reb" ready to pounce on him, and he did not slacken the horse's speed until the light of the camp fires came in view.

The command had gone into camp just in the edge of the little city of Rienzi, Miss. The following entry was made among others in the writer's diary, on this day: "Our tents and all our camp equipage were left behind, so officers and men are for once on an equality as to rations and sleeping." On the next day we receive orders to move on in the direction of Okolona, some 70 or 80 miles distant, where it was said the enemy was concentrating. Soon after starting, heavy black clouds overspread the skies, vivid lightning flashed, thunder peal after thunder peal rolled and reverberated through the cloud darkened heavens, then the water freighted clouds burst and poured their contents in fearful torrents upon us, as we were plodding thro' worse than 'dismal swamps.' Having gone some five or six miles in such elements, we bivouaced on the edge of a swamp, weary and wet, but withal full of frolic and fun. Soldiers as a class, like men in all other professions, are largely influenced by their environments, varied more or less by temporary conditions, as in the case mentioned above. It would seem that if anything on earth would or could take the fun and frolic out of a man, tho' he be a soldier, the ordeal through which our boys had just passed, and were passing, would certainly have done it. But it did not, and from their appearances and acts, one might readily suppose they would have met the whole confederacy with a whoop. But how was it, two days later with these same boys, and under much more favorable circumstances apparently? And yet, one would have inferred from their grumbling and whining that they would gladly have gone down with country just for the pleasure it would afford them to witness the sinking process, 'tis strange but true and strange but true. It was said, in effect, by his Creator, in the dawn of his creation, that man was "fearfully and wonderfully made,"[39] and the voice of the ages since then, to know has been "Know thyself."[40] But the problem remains unsolved. He thinks he knows and knows he thinks, but then have not compassed the mystery, nor even penetrated the shell that surrounds it. But this is a digression and a fruitless one too, perhaps. And to resume—(Remember the writer is now reading one of the "Towers"[41] of Samantha, the beloved wife and "pardner" of Josiah Allen, hence his too frequent effort at attempts, vain ones too, of episodin'), and now to resume again. Suppose the writer gives a sample of news received over the "grape

vine telegraph Co." in one day, while we are in camp waiting
for the escaped confederate army to turn up somewhere and
show its hand, so we can again go for it. He kept a record
of much of the news, especially war news that daily floated
through our camp when the boys had nothing else to do but
hear, magnify and report it. In looking over his army note
book for the first few days after the evacuation of Corinth,
he finds it full of the thousand and one rumors that were
daily peddled through the camp. It is safe to say that these
rumors have had Richmond the confederate capital, and
Memphis, captured and as many times as there were devils
cast out of Mary of Magdala, [42] and according to the same
source the rebels who left Corinth so unceremoniously, or as
Mrs. Samantha Allen would put, "unbeknown" to us, have
been since then on all sides of us, front, rear, and flanks just
as often. It was fortunate for us that the "Johnnies" did
not materialize on the "four sides" of us, "all to wunst," in
the comprehensive language of Mrs. Samantha A., for at
that event the relations of the two armies might have been
reversed. These contradictory rumors did however serve one
good purpose; they warded off the tendency to the "blues"
a disease prevalent in camp when the boys had nothing to
do, but think of mother and "the girl I left behind me." A
fighting or a marching army don't breed the disease. The
rumored fall of Richmond would raise a shout, while a
contradictory one would produce a fit of swearing, and
either one of these spasms would root out the "Blue Dill"
as long as it was in motion. (he means the army, and not
the other thing).

The army was chasing around more or less, and it might
have been chasing after the enemy, if so, it was so long
after, that it would take a Kit Carson or a Sitting Bull to
tell whether or not, we were on any trail at all—of the
Johnnies' make. The 25th Ill. is a tramping regiment, that

is it has been on the chase of some sort or other, ever since its organization. The writer's notes for Sunday, June 8, 1862, say: "For the first time in three months, divine services were held in the regiment." The scarcity of the services have been due to the fact that we have been on the go, every day, nearly especially on Sundays, which reminds the writer of another fact in army life as it will also do to every old soldier, in the volunteer service at least, and that is that Sunday was a general "clean up" day, and therefore the busiest day in the week.

Well, well, the chase is about over, and "catchings" have been few. Davis' Division finally went into camp near Corinth, and then remained, until Aug. 4, 1862, when it, or the larger part of it, went on the "Bay Springs expedition" and it never again returned to this section of the war's theater. In Oct. following the confederates under Gen. Sterling Price returned and attempted to retake Corinth, but was gloriously thrashed by Rosecrans.

[January 2, 1903]

The Release of a Slave Woman and Her Child

Between Eastport [43] on the Tennessee River, at the mouth of Bear creek and Iuka, [44] some 8 or 10 miles south and about midway between the two points, there stood at the time mentioned above the dwelling—a plain, old-fashioned and unpretentious and unpainted structure—of a small southern planter by the name of Thompson. He had passed his three-score-and-ten years, but was well preserved, hale, hearty and spry, a fair specimen of the better class of citizens of northern Mississippi.

A small branch of clear running water wound its serpentine course through the premises and bordering both sides of its banks and near the mansion was a beautiful grove of native grown trees, making an inviting place for an army to camp, which the teamsters who were engaged in hauling army supplies stored at Eastport to Iuka and other places at the front, were not slow in appropriating for that purpose. The mansion stood near the main road and in plain view from the grove.

The muleteers and their mounted escorts had in passing the house frequently seen a woman standing at one of the windows in an upper story gazing at them. And they also discovered that the window was barred with wooden slats nailed on the outside. This created a suspicion in the minds of the blue coats that the woman was confined there against her will. And they were not long in coming to the conclusion an investigation should be instituted and the facts ascertained. And they proceeded at once to act upon this conclusion.

Selecting from the grove surrounding their camp a tree or sapling suitable for the purpose—one full of limbs and straight—they soon converted it into an "Indian ladder" by trimming off the limbs so as to leave enough for a step or foothold next to the body of the tree. This, when night had cast her somber mantle over hill and dale, and all was quiet at the Thompson mansion, they carried in silence and put in position under the grated window. Then one of their number ascended the improvised ladder and found the occupant at the window watching the proceedings closely as the darkness would permit. She proved to be a colored woman, a slave, some twenty years or more old. She was mulatto, well formed, and well informed, too, her condition considered. Her hair was dark and wavey, not kinky, and her eyes were faultless, as the novelist would say, but the

39

writer is compelled, in the interest of truth, to say he can't name the color. She, when the ladder climber asked why she was thus confined, stated that her husband, who was also a slave belonging to her master had recently "skipped " out with a squad of blue coats and her master fearing she would follow him had adopted that method to prevent it.

[July 6, 1902]

She had one child, a boy some three years old, a bright little fellow who was in the room with her. She said when questioned that she was anxious to be released from her imprisonment, and from bondage as well, so the slats were quickly removed from the window, and she and her child were carefully assisted to the ground and the next morning were taken by her rescuers to Eastport and left at post headquarters, where she was employed as a cook and soon proved that she was not a stranger to the "art culinary" by any means.

From absolute knowledge the writer, after a lapse of forty years is ready and willing to assert that her cooking would not suffer in any particular in comparison with the best efforts of any aunty "Chloe" or "Dinah," or any other aunty, who ever flourished and ruled the kitchen and mastered the intricacies of the culinary department in the most noted mansion on the best ordered plantation in the beautiful southland befo' the wah, suh.

The name of the woman, and "cooking prodigy"— her first name, he means—cannot now be called to mind, further than that she was Thompson's "yaller gal," in the local vernacular. But her dinners cooked and served in the old warehouse that stood on the banks of the Tennessee, just below Chicsaw Bluff, [45] are as fresh in the mind of the writer to-day as they were when partaken of in 1862 because of the very marked contrast between them and "hard tack and sow belly."

A few days after the escape of the "yaller gal" and her kid, her master—that was—struck her trail and followed it to the end. She saw him approaching and with motherly instinct, seized her boy and darted below, like a shot—the building being a two-story one—and awaited developments. This left in the office and post headquarters only the wife of Capt. Allen and the writer, when Mr. Thompson entered. Mrs. Allen who was not long from the land of "Boggs and Brawls" was at this time visiting her husband. She was a short heavy set woman, red hair and ready wit, with a glib tongue, with which to use it, and like the average son of the "Green Isle," was fully ready, at any time for a "wake" or a war, as the incident following will demonstrate. The old gentleman upon entering the room and before taking the offered seat, asked in a somewhat haughty manner if a "yaller gal and her child were here?" Mrs. Allen, without answering his question, asked quickly how the matter concerned him, and he at once replied that he had lost a gal and her child and he understood they were here, and he wished to find them and take them home. He then started toward the stairs leading down to the basement, whither the chattels had just gone. At this stage in the proceeding the now thoroughly aroused Mrs. Allen made a dash for her husband's sword, which was hanging on a nail driven into one of the posts of the building, she took it down and unsheathing it in a jiffy she quickly stepped in front of the searcher for a runaway gal and her child and told him pointedly and in the rich brogue of her race, that if he attempted to molest the woman and her child she would thrust him through with the sword, at the same time making a few awkward movements with a weapon that she had never before handled perhaps. Thompson halted, but did not seem to be alarmed in the least. Mrs. Allen kept up her sword movements and gesticulations, interspersed with flashes of native wit for a time, and then subsided. The old man then said in an apparently mollified tone of voice that he did not wish to violate any military rule or order, but he would have been pleased to see the gal and especially the boy. Mrs. Allen retorted "that he could not do." Thompson then left the office and disturbed the quiet of the post and the captain's wife's temper never again.

Now let us for a moment see what has become of the woman and child who had made such a masterly retreat to the basement at the approach of their legal master. As soon as the contention between Mrs. Allen and the slave hunter had ceased, the writer who had been the only witness to the "war of words" between them, went below to see what had become of the hunted woman and child. Before relating what he saw and heard it may be well to briefly describe the building, especially the basement in which he had found them.

As has before been stated the building was a large old styled barn framed structure, of two stories, constructed and at this time used for a steamboat freight house, and was located upon the bank of the river—Tennessee—the riverside of the building being flush with the bank which was quite deep and precipitous, so that one standing in the door facing the river could easily jump into the turbid waters, and it was just there with her babe pressed to heaving breast, the river at her feet, where the writer found the "yaller gal" standing, a sight to move the heart of a stone! As he approached her, she turning her face toward him said excitedly, "are they going to give us up?" He replied "I think not," and she apparently, not hearing his answer, continued "I'll never go back, I and"—speaking the name of her child which the writer has forgotten—"will go to the bottom of the river together if they attempt to send us back to the old massa," and her looks and actions indicated clearly that such was her purpose, and it is the writer's firm conviction, based upon his previous and subsequent knowledge of the woman that had her then legal master approached her when he made the attempt, she would have leaped with her child into the turbid waters of the Tennessee, and gone down beneath the waves to a watery grave.

This incident is not a fancy tale, is not far-fetched or overdrawn. It occurred just at the time and in the place and manner as has been related. And by the way such incidents, while perhaps, somewhat rare did occasionally occur among the slaves of the south, especially during the later years of the life of the institution, when the principle of and the desire for freedom had become more generally diffused among the slaves—the period just preceding the war.

A few days after this event, the army supplies stored at Eastport having been removed, and the enemy getting too thick and near, added to the further fact that the place had only a small force—a detachment—of the 39th Ohio Infantry—guarding it. Beside which the enemies' cavalry, regular partisan rangers, were filling the woods all around, threatening to make it hot for the yanks, it was decided that the Post should be abandoned, which was done, and in due time Allen and wife and the gal and kid, and the clerk turned up safely at Corinth by way of Iuka Springs, Miss. Mrs. Allen was about to return north and desired to take with her the woman and child and you may be sure the woman was in a perfect frenzy to accompany her.

This was before, only a few days however, the issuing of the preliminary Emancipation Proclamation by President Lincoln—Sept 22, 1862. So it was not an easy matter at times to get a fugitive slave through the lines to go north. Altho Gen. Ben Butler had attempted in 1861 to apply the distinction and rule of contrabands of war, to the slaves of Southerners, when they fell into our hands. But as Mr. Lincoln's policy thus far in the prosecution of the war had been strictly on constitutional lines Old Ben's pleas were not officially endorsed, [46] tho perhaps at times practiced on the sly, by officers not in sympathy with the "peculiar institution."

The writer being of the anti-slavery cult, from way back, and was then wearing the "blue" because of this fact and believed as old Ben did, and was therefore fully of the opinion that a person, especially a woman, who preferred death to slavery, was entitled to her freedom in a country that boasted of the liberty of its citizens, and he determined to do what he could to assist her in getting out of a bondage she dreaded more than she did death and a grave beneath the waters.

[July 13, 1902]

The brave, generous and humane General James B. McPherson at this time had charge of transportation matters in and around Corinth, so the writer went to the General direct in order to find out what would be done for the colored refugee and child. He found the General with his hands clasped behind pacing up and down the track of the old Mobile & Ohio railroad upon which was then standing a mixed train, the puffing and hissing of the engine, with its head to the north, indicating that it was now ready for duty. And, by the way, it was the train that Mrs. Allen was about to board for her northern home. The writer approached and saluted the General, which he recognized, and stopped his pace. The writer then briefly told him what he knew of the woman, her own wish and that of Mrs. Allen in the matter, which seemed to interest the General. But he in reply stated that he had no authority to give her transportation or even a pass, but he thought if she got aboard of the train no one would molest her. "I'll see to that," said he. And his word settled the matter, for he never went back on it. Thanking him, the writer hastened to give the result of his efforts to the parties most interested and anxiously awaiting his return. The information he had to impart so elated the slave woman when she began to realize that the goal of her dearest wishes and most earnest prayer was about to be reached that she was fairly beside herself. But the puffing engine and shrill whistle gave warning to all who were going to step aboard or be left. So there was not time for delay even to indulge in the great joy of prospective liberty from the worst form of human slavery, which seemed to permeate her entire being and gave expression in ejaculatory prayers and tears. The train was reached and boarded in due time and was soon rolling its freight—human and otherwise—toward a country never cursed by the shackles and rod of the soulless slave driver, north of Mason's and Dixon's line.

The writer has never seen or heard a word in relation to the woman and her child since the day he assisted them in getting aboard the train in Corinth, Miss., about the middle of September, 1862. He hopes she arrived safely with Capt. Allen's wife at her home in the grand old prairie State, and that after the "cruel war was over" in which, no doubt, he took an honorable part in the defense of the flag and in securing his own emancipation from a heartless servitude, her husband in due time rejoined his brave and fearless wife, who barred doors and windows had alone prevented her from the attempt to follow him when he first "lef de old plantation and Massa Thompson and de ole Missus" in defiance of the laws then existing and became a hunted refugee and who, after escaping from "durance vile," [47] and was followed by her then legal master of her body and its

Daniel O. Root

issue, would have given her own life and that of her own child rather than return to her shackles and shame, that many happy days and years have been added to their re-united lives, that the kid Jim, and any other additions that may have come to the family freeborn has or have grown into useful and prosperous citizens. Whether such have been the results or not, the writer is proud of the part he was permitted to take in giving freedom to a mother and child just a little before the great and martyred Lincoln, with a few strokes of the pen, gave freedom to their entire race.

The record shows that Capt. Allen's residence at the time of this enlistment was _____[left blank, probably Pike County], Ill., and there is where his wife with her colored protégé and her boy evidently landed and there, or in that vicinity, doubtless Thompson's "yaller gal" and child, whom dame rumor charged sustained other relations to their master than that of legal servitude, settled and perhaps still remains. It matters not, however. The declaration of this untutored woman, born and reared under the debasing influence and practices of slavery, as it existed in the beautiful Southland anterior to the war, that she preferred death to slavery and its consequences, and was on the point of verifying this declaration, is as much entitled to be handed down to coming ages, tho' uttered by a bond woman, as are the utterances of great moral truth by men who have reached Fame's exalted pinnacles, for they, like the genealogy of the King of Salem, are "without beginning of days or end of life"—eternal.[48] But here this chapter endeth.

[July 20, 1902]

46

CHAPTER THREE

THE BAY SPRINGS EXPEDITION

Before the March

During the spring and summer of 1862, the regiment—25th Ill. Vol. Infy.—was a part of Gen. Jeff C. Davis' Division, which was operating in and around Corinth, Miss. Of this regiment, made up entirely of companies from Champaign, Coles, Douglas, Edgar, Iroquois and Vermilion counties, the writer was a member. But in August, 1862 when the regiment was sent north to assist in checking the advance of the confederates into Kentucky, endangering the safety of Louisville, if not Cincinnati also, he was left at Iuka on detached service, by order of Gen. Rosecrans, commander of the army of the Mississippi. If he had not have been on such service at the time, he could not have gone with his regiment, however, for the reason that he was "housed up" or "tented up" with as bad a case of poisoned feet, as one need wish to find, if on the lookout for a perfect type of such a disease. He may tell later of how and where he caught the disease, or rather how it caught him, for it was on an important night march, when the "catching" occurred. It may be proper right here to state, as some of the incidents he may relate, happened after the regiment to which he belonged had left the section of country in which he claimed they had occurred, that the writer was never with his regiment after it left for Kentucky as noted above. He remained on detached duty in the vicinity of Corinth until his discharge from the army, Oct. 18, 1862, for "disability." So, he and his command were somewhat widely separated for sometime before he left the service.

He will also state that he kept a continuous diary of his soldier life, as he does not have to rely altogether on memory for the details of his "tales," such as they are.

The event, or rather the succession of events, he will now attempt to relate, occurred on what was known as the "Bay Springs Expedition." Bay Springs was a small village, on a small stream in the northern part of Itawamba county, Miss., south east some 25 miles of Jacinto. Jacinto was at this time the county seat of Tishomingo Co., which embraced territory now comprising the counties of Alcorn, Prentiss and Tishomingo, in the north-east corner of the state of Mississippi. The village contained a cotton mill run by water power, which made the yarn but did not weave the cloth. It was also the headquarters of a band of guerrillas, [49] that was annoying our outposts, so it was decided to make an effort to capture or disperse it.

Gen. Robert E. Mitchell, a Kansas Jayhawker, [50] who was temporarily in charge of Gen. Jeff C. Davis' division of the army of the Mississippi, had command of the expedition, Davis himself being away on a leave of absence during which he and Gen. Nelson, between whom there existed some matters of difference, met at the Galt House in Louisville, Ky., the result of which was the death of Nelson, at the hands of Davis. The expedition consisted of the 25th and 59th Ill. Inf., 22nd Ind. Infy., and parts of the 6th Kansas and 7th Ill. Cavalry and four pieces of artillery, being the First Brigade of Davis' Division.

And it included the writer also, who carried a musket that was as dangerous at one end as at the other in use, otherwise it was quite harmless. He was further encumbered with a cartridge box in which were 40 rounds of ammunition, a knapsack with nothing in it but a few writing materials. A haversack, in which there was supposed to be three days of cooked rations and a canteen, altogether giving him the appearance, he now imagines, of a Jew pack-peddler and a game hunter combined. But he then felt he was every inch a soldier. Let him quote a few lines from his diary of Aug. 3rd (Sunday) 1862, the day before the starting of the expedition.

"We were not attacked last night, nor were we otherwise disturbed."

"We are looking for and greatly needing the paymaster."

"Orders came in the p.m. to prepare three days cooked rations in haversacks and be ready to march to-morrow morning early."

"Where we are going is a question easier asked than answered."

Now, if you will let him, the writer will paraphrase a little upon the first item quoted. "We were not attacked last night." This would indicate that an attack was expected during the night, but such was by no means the case. The evening before Gen. Asboth who was encamped at Rienzi, some few miles from our camp, had sent a message to Gen. Mitchell, post haste, informing him that the enemy in force, was hovering around his—Asboth's—outposts, and for him, Mitchell, to hold his force in readiness to assist in repelling the attack which would doubtless be made that night. Such messages were so common from Asboth and had always proved so groundless, that they had ceased to do aught for us but create a spirit of mirth and jeering among the boys, and whenever we knew that Asboth expected to be attacked, we felt assured that the enemy was giving us a "wide berth" and we could forage or sleep without fear of him. If his courage had been equal to his caution—and he was a "fighting Dutchman"—he would himself have been a match single handed for all the rebs that were threatening to attack him on the aforesaid night. Asboth, it seemed, was never so happy as when he was about to be attacked, and could get his own command, and all adjacent commands "to fall into line" at the hour of midnight and stand there until his scare would pass off about daylight.

[August 1, 1902]

Soldiers Experience Intense Suffering from the Heat

The expedition was to start from Camp Clear creek, near Jacinto, early in the morning of August 4th, and the compound was drawn up in marching order. But from some cause the starting was delayed some time. Finally, however, at about 10:30 a.m. the command to move out was given, and the boys who had been in camp several days, glad to be on the move again started off at a brisk step to the tune of "The Girl I Left Behind Me," or some other one equally inspiring.

The day was intensely hot, a record breaker in fact, and the commanding officers being mounted did not realize the fact in time to avert serious results, for before little more than one mile had been gone over the men began to literally fall or drop out of the ranks, overcome by the fearful heat, and before this condition of affairs reached the officer in command, Gen. Mitchell, who was in the advance, between 35 and 40 men lay helpless along the road passed over.

The command was halted, of course, and the ambulances gathered up the stricken boys, most of whom never fell into the ranks again, and no martial strains or bugle blasts could "e'er awake them to glory again." The writer tumbled out of the line and came down under a big oak tree standing by the road side. That is, he was not so far gone but that he could select a good place to light, and by the way, it was the first time he was ever forced out of the ranks on a march because he could go no further, and the only time. Northern Mississippi, you know, alternates between ridges and swamps. The white sand and clay soil of the ridges through the hot season, during the day, became heated like an oven. The nights as a rule are cool and pleasant, however, rendering some compensation for the day's extra heat.

The entire command remained in the shade of trees that lined the road, a short distance east of Jacinto, until just before sunset, when the march was resumed at a much slower pace than at the outset, however.

Our objective point was to the southeast, but in order to throw the enemy off his guard we took a course due east, as if going to Iuka. Having gone four or five miles the command was halted along side of a nice field of corn, in prime roasting ear condition and then, Mitchell came riding back along our lines shouting over and over again, "Boys, do you see this corn field? Charge on it." And charge they did and soon, at least 2,000 men were either gathering the succulent roasting ears or preparing the fire and water for their cooking. During the eating process the General passed around among the boys telling them to eat a plenty and fill their haversacks, for they would have to march a good part of the night.

The discipline and social characteristics of Mitchell were so different from those of Gen. Davis that they evoked remarks from the boys decidedly more complimentary to his qualities than to those of Davis. Davis was trained in the school of practical experience among regulars and every whit a soldier, while Mitchell lacked their training, perhaps, and was more a man than a soldier, but he pleased the soldiers better.

After the corn feast was over the night march began, it being then about 8 o'clock p.m., and the heat less oppressive, but the roads were fearfully dusty. But instead of an all night's march we went into camp near a swamp at about 10 o'clock p.m., some 12 miles from our starting point.

The next morning, quoting from the writer's notes made at the time, "we were early on the road, but went but a short distance when we were halted and remained in the shade at a place called Thompson's Cross Roads until evening, when we turned south and east about seven miles and bivouaced in a lane, the dust and fleas being about six inches deep. The writer hopes no reader of the INDEPENDENT will call in question this statement relating to the dust and fleas. Remember it was forty years ago, and is now outlawed, and then it was made by a soldier who sometimes shoots wide of the truth as he does of the enemy. If he were to qualify this statement at this late date he would simply say that the dust was deep and fleas thick as hops, which may or may not be six inches, you know.

We were aroused the next morning before day and were ready to march by sun-rise. And here the writer will again draw from his diary, for Wednesday, August 6th, 1862, which says: "Two of the enemy's pickets were taken in last night and five or six horses. About sunrise we started on quick time for Bay Springs, distant some seven miles, and the column did not halt until it arrived there. The cavalry being in the advance, charged on the pickets posted just outside the village and took several prisoner, the rest falling back upon their main force, a mile or so below the town, followed by our cavalry, a running fire being kept up. But the guerrillas, when their chased pickets came in, left in the greatest confusion, and haste. A few shells were thrown into the woods surrounding the place with the effect only of frightening the citizens out of their wits and houses as well, leaving their morning meals on the tables untouched largely, which the invading Yankees soon appropriated to their own use, without thanks, and without rendering an equivalent. In fact, the village was completely looted. The one store—a store of general merchandise—was entered and its contents distributed among the boys as far as it would go. The writer's trophy consisted of one pair of women's shoes. No. 8's, with high heels. And these he did not get from the wrecked store, but from a comrade who had pillaged a private house and procured two pairs of ladies' shoes and was generous enough to divide with the writer who otherwise would have had no booty to bear away from the field of strife and to boast of in after years to his grandchildren.

The cotton mill was despoiled of enough of its machinery to render it useless as a yarn spinner for a while at least.

As the shades of the evening were falling upon the deserted and wrecked village nestling between the hills that were hiding its inhabitants from its despoiler, they--the despoilers—were forming the ranks preparatory to leaving on their return trip. The expedition had succeeded in its purposes and was departing in high spirits back to camp or to new fields of action.

We marched until after midnight and then were halted and told to rest until morning, which we proceeded to do without coaxing and had a soft bed of dust and fleas to lay on, and we slept well, too.

This was the night when the writer got his feet poisoned, an allusion to which had heretofore been made, the result of an experiment in "bare foot" marching and coming in contact with poison vines and weeds, the effect of which was as bad as a flesh wound from a rebel rifle. He is therefore justified in saying that, so far as he knows, he is the only man in the expedition that can lay claim to having been wounded. Near the place where the head of the column halted, as noted above, was a farm house occupied by a staunch old rebel with a grown-up family. General Mitchell and some of the other officers aroused the family and entered the house and passed themselves off for Gen. Price and staff of the Confederate army, who were known to be not far away. This, of course, gave them access to not only the best of everything in the house but also their confidence. And without much prompting or circumlocution they very soon got all out of this old "Secesh" they cared to know. They learned that it was he who had given the guerrillas we had gone after warning of our movement by sending one of his sons on a by-path with the information. So the guerrillas were on the lookout for us. The old man was taken into custody, but the writer never knew what was done with him.

In the morning, just as we were on the point of starting in the direction of our old camp, orders came for the entire command to turn east and go to Iuka, so we filed to the right as soon as we struck a road that would permit such a movement. After going some five or six miles we went into camp by a small creek, our supply train having overtaken us there.

Scared While on Picket Duty

That night the writer was detailed for picket duty and during the night the incident following occurred: Our detail numbered 23, one of whom was a sergeant, who had charge of the squad. And we were stationed along the road we had just passed over, about a mile from camp. There were three guard posts formed—an outer, an inner and a reserved one. And it was so arranged that none of the men need go on duty but once during the night. And we went on duty by twos, that is, two occupied a station at the same time.

The writer's turn to go on duty came at about 11 o'clock p.m., and his fellow guardsman was a member of his own company—George Sargent, a nephew of the late Snowden Sargent, [51] for whom Sargent Township, this county, was named. And he is still living. Our station was the outer one and close to the junction of two roads. The road upon which we were posted ran from some distance through a dense grove of small timber, and underbrush and was for some distance without a crook in it. The night was clear and the moon at its full, and where it shone on the road or other objects it was as bright and clear almost as the sun light, but in the shade the darkness was Egyptian. A few minutes after we had taken our position, which was at the roadside in the shade of a clump of trees with a dense foliage, hiding us from observation so completely as if we were in the bowels of the earth, we heard the clatter of a horse's hoofs, to the south, seemingly on a road at right angles to the one on which we were posted. And, judging from the sound, it would intersect or cross our road a few rods to the west of our station and outside our lines. Was it a horse with or without a rider? was our first query. And the next one was, if it had a rider was he friend or foe?

[August 8, 1902]

Our queries and consequent suspense would soon be unraveled, for the sound of the hoofs were becoming more distinct and we could hear the coughing or sneezing of the animal, as if attempting to expel the dust from his throat and nostrils as he sped along.

To say that the two sentinels were about this time excited is putting it mildly indeed. It would be much nearer the truth to say they were scared. The writer, at least, was, and will at this distance from the time of the incident freely confess it. They kept their wits, however, sufficiently to enable them to agree upon their mode of procedure in the event the horse had a rider and should attempt to pass their post. Sargent was to do the challenging and the writer was to manipulate his musket if necessary. And this by the way, was just as he wanted it, for he could trust his gun going off much better than he could his tongue. You know when one's heart and tongue are in the mouth at the same time there is no telling what might happen—to the tongue. But the horse with his clatter was coming on apace, and so were the emotions of the guardsmen as they stood trembling in the shade and in their boots. But they kept an eye on the spot where they judged the horse would first strike the road, all the same.

It is said "the darkest hour is just before day" and we found it in this case, for the moment the horse and his rider, for he had one, entered the road and turned toward us, our sense of duty as a soldier asserted itself and we were ready to do or die. And as soon as the rider got within the prescribed distance we quickly stepped to the center of the road, when Mr. Sargent commanded him to halt and at the same instant the writer pulled back the hammer on his musket, the action making a clicking sound that the horseman could easily hear, and held his "piece in position to fire." The rider halted and so suddenly, too, that he came near being thrown over the horse's head and the horse thrown upon his haunches. The challenger then asked "who goes there?" And the challenged replied instantly: "A friend without the countersign."

As soon as the rider spoke we recognized him, so further precaution was not necessary. He was the hospital steward [52] of our regiment and had been out to see a sick woman. Just after we had gone into camp a citizen came to get a physician to go and see his wife who was sick, his home doctor being in hiding from the "Lincoln hirelings." None of the surgeons would go. So the hospital steward of the 25th Ill. Infy. volunteered his services and went and one, at least of the results of his going was the incident just attempted to be related. He had gone out before the guards had been posted or the countersign given out. So he got as badly scared in getting back to camp, as he had been the means of frightening the two sentinels.

At day light the pickets were all called into the reserve post, to await the order for their relief from duty. But the relief was slow in coming. We heard bugles in camp nearly a mile away, sound the different calls, and finally the call to "fall in" came wafting on the morning breeze to our ears, and we became convinced that we had been overlooked, but we dare not leave our post without orders. The sun came up in splendor and began his climb toward mid heavens, and still we were forgotten and were also getting hungry, for our "hard tack and sow belly," had been left in camp, and was then, no doubt, getting farther away from us with the moving column. Restlessly and anxiously we waited, for in addition to our increasing hunger, we were in danger of being "gobbled up" and taken in by some roving band of Roddy's Rangers "on mischief bent," [53] who were in the habit of doing such tricks. "in season and out of season." [54] But fortunately just before "forbearance ceased to be a virtue,"[55] and patience became exhausted, an orderly on lathering horse, with the long coveted order for our recall, came and we at once started in pursuit of the Bay Springs expedition and our "hard tack" and his twin sister "sow belly." But after going on "quick step" for a mile or so, it dawned upon at least three of the ex-pickets, that if their breakfast did not come until the moving column was overtaken it would, at the very best, turn out to be a late supper, and another thing was equally as apparent to them, and that was that it would be a waste of time to attempt to get anything like a square, home like meal at any house on the road over which 2,000 soldiers had just passed, anyone of whom had a relish no doubt for an old fashioned meal. So the writer and his picket mate—Sargent—and a comrade whose name cannot now be recalled, concluded to take the first cross road or by path and follow it until a dwelling was reached that could supply the wherewith to satisfy the cravings of these badly depleted stomachs.

[August 15, 1902]

Catching a Tartar

A few moments after this conclusion was reached a by-path was discovered diverging toward the southwest nearly in the opposite direction to that we were going. Fresh tracks of a wagon appearing in this by-road was an additional bid for them to explore the regions to which it led. So they turned into it with the results that here follow.

First saying, however, that hunger, like forbidden love, sometimes leads beyond the bounds of prudence and safety, as will be seen later on. Less than one-half mile from the main road the trio came to a small enclosure in which stood a log cabin, surrounded on three sides by growing corn. A woman with a milk pail in hand was just emerging from the cabin door as the three hungry breakfast hunters approached the fence in front of the house. The writer, who had been made spokesman for the "squad," if, indeed, three constitute a squad, asked her, after the usual compliments of the morning had been passed, what the charges were for breakfast. Without answering the question she asked, "Are you Federal or Confederate soldiers?" He replied, "We are Federals." She then said, "Boys, I am glad to see you. You are the first Federals I ever saw. We are Unionist but dare not say anything. We are poor but will divide with you. Go in the house." But she kept on talking all the same, the purport of which was that her husband, who was still in bed, came in during the night from Eastport whither he had gone for salt, and that was why she had slept so late into morning. But it is not necessary to follow her farther. She seemed to be honest and truthful, if she did belong to the "poor white trash."

The spokesman then asked her if there was not a disunion family near that could furnish the desired meals without seriously depleting his larder. And she frankly admitted that there was one of that stripe living not far away, who had two sons and a son-in-law in the rebel army. And she pointed out the house, which was in sight just across an intervening swamp. And also directed us where to cross the swamp to reach the house without going a round about way. So after bidding the Unionist lady good-day they left to try their luck with a disunion one. Following the directions given they had little trouble in getting over the quagy swamp. In ascending the ridge, the base of which came down to the edge of the swamp, one of the boys needlessly, foolishly, imprudently discharged his musket, the report of which echoed and revibrated [sic] from ridge to ridge with sufficient volume and distinctness to arouse the entire neighborhood. And as they were near the house they were seeking and were approaching it from the rear, the lady of the house had heard the report and doubtless supposing it came from the gun of some skulking, treacherous ranger who had sent a bullet into the heart of some straggling blue coat, came out the back way, all aglow with the expectation of meeting her friend, the murderer, but instead met the three hungry and, by the way, dirty breakfast hunters of the Federal army at the rear gate. She was perhaps sixty years old, medium size, complexion dark yellowish peculiar to women of the south of the middle classes. Her hair, once black, was then streaked with gray. And her eyes were still dark and snappish, showing that the vinegar had not all yet gone out of her composition and was still able, from appearances, to keep up her tilts with her liege lord and not miss getting in the last word every time.

The writer, who was still spokesman, realized before a word was spoken that he had caught or was desperately near to catching a tartar. [56] But hunger was goading him and his comrades on to desperate deeds if necessary. So there could be no retreat, and he ventured to say, "Good morning, madam." And she, still under the impression that she was in the presence of her friends, answered the salutation without hesitancy and at the same time advancing closer to the gate as if to get a better view of her visitors. The writer then said, "Madam, can you get us something to eat? We have had no breakfast." She replied by saying, "You are Confederate soldiers, I believe." And he answered, "We are not." It might be said just here that they could easily have passed for Confederates. They had been marching and lying in the dust for four or five days, and sweating freely, the dirt had adhered to clothes and skin until it was difficult to tell the complexion of either, so they could easily have fooled the old lady and it might not have been committing an unpardonable sin if it had been done.

The answer of the writer that they were not rebel soldiers wrought a sudden and radical change in the looks and demeanor of their anticipated and finally enforced hostess. The venom of her ire knew no bounds. She belched it out like old Mount Pelee [57] did his lava when at his best, winding up her tirade in an hysterical conglomeration of curses, cries, prayers and tears. Before the hysteria stage, however, was fully developed, when she was doubtless getting on a full head of steam for the coming climax, she avowed that the intruders upon her rights and privileges were no more nor less than "mudsills," "Lincoln hirelings," "nigger lovers, and thieves and robbers as well," and that they had no right in her house nor on her premises.

When she had exhausted the vocabulary of epithets and abuse at her command, and her tongue could wag no longer until rest should restore its power to wag again, the writer seeing a chance to slip in a word, and being in a good frame of mind brought about by her violent evolutions, said to her without mincing a word, "Madam, we propose now to have something to eat, peacefully if we can, forcefully if we must, and you must choose which it shall be."

[August 22, 1902]

This statement seemed to stagger the old lady and she turned her back to her persecutors, mumbling in a subdued voice that it had come to a pretty pass when a person could not control her own affairs, and started toward the house, but suddenly stopped and about faced, and said, with a look of half defiance and half surrender, she said, "You will pay for what you get, I suppose?" And the writer, who was still smarting over the lashing he had received, retorted with directness and force, "Not a cent, madam. Your treatment merits no such consideration at our hands," which remark did not have a soothing effect upon the nerves of the unwilling landlady. She then again turned her steps toward the house, the three dirty and hungry Federals following in Indian file.

The house was a typical residence of the middle class of citizens of the state, consisting of a double building, one story and an attic, connected by a side hall open at both ends and extending the whole length of the building, and was used by the family and guests as a sitting room in the heated season of the year, doors leading from it into the kitchen, which was one side of it, and into the dwelling proper or living room, which was on the opposite side.

Sitting in this entry or hall when the old lady and her Yankee tormentors entered was a woman whom our unwilling hostess introduced to the Yankees as her daughter, and she looked it, too. And providing her intruders with chairs went into the kitchen to prepare or give orders for the preparation of the meal demanded.

Left alone with the daughter the "blue coats," notwithstanding their long fasting and consequent hunger, attempted to get some fun or amusement out of, or at her expense, by cracking jokes, boasting of superiority in looks, dress and valor, of the Northern over the Southern army, and predicting the speedy suppression of the rebellion. But the writer will not say that the final outcome exceeded their expectations. The truth is she proved to be a chip off the old block—the maternal end of it at least—and was a real clipper, with a tongue loose at both ends, having the peculiar faculty of using both ends, apparently, at the same time, and getting in the last word, without effort, every time you bet.

The announcement that breakfast was ready sounded a truce to the fun and flaying, more than half of which—especially the fun—the daughter evidently was enjoying to the full.

In their haste and eagerness to appease their pressing hunger, the trio in obeying the summons to breakfast left their guns leaning against the wall where they had been sitting, and within arms length of the wife of a rebel soldier, who was in full sympathy with the cause for which he was fighting and who was liable, at any moment to be joined by her mother whose sympathies run in the same channel, all of which the writer fully realized before taking his seat at the table, but did not care to betray his fears in the presence of the old lady who was waiting on the table. Fortunately he was so seated at the table that by leaning back and craning his neck he could see the gun—his own--farthest one from the daughter. When the mother had served the coffee, and the yanks had begun a vigorous onslaught upon the rather sparsely filled table, she retreated to the hall and with her daughter and three loaded guns, she or they, was or were, if she or they had been so disposed, master or masters of the situation.

The writer called the attention of his comrades to the act so unsoldierly and reckless, especially in the midst of enemies. Just then the old lady returned, and having heard something of the conversation, or guessing at it, she remarked, "Boys you can see," pointing in the direction of their guns, "that we do not wish to do you harm, for we could have done so if we had." Sargent replied, "Two women with three shots would have had a d----d hard time taking three men with twelve shots."

Sargent and the other soldiers had revolvers with them, nevertheless the situation of the "boys" was too far from being safe to make a good joke, and the writer did not feel at ease until he was again by the side of his old musket.

The meal over, Mrs. Rodgers—for that was the family name—said to them as they were about to leave, between sobs, prayers, and imprecations, "You are the first Federal soldiers we have seen, and you have treated us better than we expected, from what we had heard about you. And now boys I have two sons and a son-in-law in the Confederate service, and they are now prisoners of war, at Indianapolis, [58] were members of the 3rd Miss. Regiment, and were captured at Fort Donelson. I wish you would treat them as I have treated you, if you should ever meet them." Of course the "boys" promised. But the writer hinted to her that the "good part" [59] of the treatment they had received from her had been enforced and therefore not meritorious, but she not heeding the attempted thrust of the writer, went on to say that she had a letter written to her boys that she very much desired to have mailed to them, that she had for days been watching for a chance to have it sent. The Yanks informed her that they would take her letter and see that it was duly mailed.

And the writer is glad to say that he knows the trust was conscientiously carried out as promised. The sun was now in mid heavens when the three Feds, with appetites appeased and the humor of their unwilling hostess somewhat mollified, started in search of the Bay Springs expedition, which the writer's notes for Friday, Aug. 6th, 1862 say: "Got into Iuka Springs at 12 o'clock m. and went into camp in a nice grove at the east side of the village." Just outside the gate they met the old man Rodgers coming in from the direction of the road which the expedition had that morning passed. He had doubtless been on the lookout for something that he could turn over to the interest of the Southern Confederacy.

They were glad, you may be assured, that he had delayed his return until they had secured possession of their arms again. The old man, had, seemingly a much quieter tongue than that of his "better half, " but was a full-fledged "Secesh" all the same.

The next day, right in this neighborhood, a member of the 21st Ill. Infy. (Grant's old regiment) who lived in the neighborhood of old Bloomfield, Edgar county, was shot and instantly killed while riding on a sutler's wagon by a skulking ranger in ambush.[60]

And just here, if the reader will excuse the digression, the writer will state that a few days after this event he was assigned to duty in the provost marshall's office at Iuka, as noted elsewhere in these "Reminiscences," and he well remembers that two of the prominent men of this vicinity were arrested by the military authorities, and brought before the provost, charged with disloyalty and harboring the sneaking skulking guerrillas in their deviltry, the killing of the soldier just mentioned being one of the causes leading to their arrest. They were paroled upon giving bonds of $10,000 each amply secured, for their good behavior and loyalty, and were required to report once a week to the provost in person. The papers in these cases were drawn up by the writer, for which they were charged $5.00 each, one paying in gold, the other in a five dollar note on a bank in Nashville, Tenn., whose notes circulated at par, whether the city was in the possession of the Federals or Confederates. So it must have been a union bank of Feds and Confeds.

Both of these men when brought into the provost office were as badly frightened, if appearances and actions indicate anything, as it is possible for men to be, and live. They would have signed away all their earthly belongings and any rights they may have had or hoped to have in "kingdom come," if it had been demanded.

But, returning to the narrative which the writer is attempting to give of the Bay Springs expedition, and from which he digressed in order to relate the incident just closed, it will be remembered that the three ex-pickets had just left the Rodgers plantation and were turning their faces and making steps in the direction of Iuka, whither their command had gone, leaving them on the picket line. They soon reached the road over which the expedition had passed and without further mishap they reached camp, which was located in a beautiful grove just east of the village of Iuka, then known as Iuka Springs, several hours after the arrival of the main force, glad indeed to be again within the sheltering lines of the "blue coats." But he was not yet altogether out of trouble, for there was in his regiment an order in force placing every soldier who failed to get into camp, when on a march, with his company, on extra duty, unless other duties prevented. So he had scarcely stacked his arms until the orderly sergeant detailed him to go on extra duty at once. This was a direct slap in the face, indicating disobedience of military orders or the commission of some crime worthy of punishment, to be inflicted without a hearing, when he was, he thought, more entitled to have the "brass and field bands" out heading a procession of veterans to welcome his safe return to his command after his exploits on the "picket line" and his confab and whatnot with old mother Rodgers and her daughter of the same make and mold, to say nothing of his starving for some three or four mortal hours, executing the soul inspiring strains of "Behold, the Conquering Hero Comes," [61] or words to that effect.

The contrast was far too great for mortal endurance between what was and what ought to have been, and must be resented then and there—and it was. For he was not only humiliated but was angered as well, from his head to the tips of his toes. So he said, in language that needed no interpreter to understand it: "You know why he did not come into camp with the company just as well as he knows that he, himself, will not go on extra duty to-day." To this outburst, or attempted bluff, the orderly said: "Go to the major," who was at the time in command of the regiment, "and get excused." And the writer retorted: "Not much, if you please." And he said: "You'll go on duty, then."

From the very start the writer had determined that he should not go on extra duty, nor would he go to the commanding officer of the regiment and ask to be excused. He knew that there had been a gross blunder made, to say the least, and that some one was responsible for it. The fact that a body of men—twenty-three in number—without a commissioned officer with them, should be placed in the important position of outpost pickets, in the enemy's country, when the forces to which they belong were on the move and not in camp is unmilitary and bad. But when they are left at their posts for hours after their command are upon the march before the order for their relief comes, is an indication of gross neglect if not criminal carelessness. And the writer knew it, or thought he did, so he felt safe in the position taken by him, and he even went further in his refusal to obey an order so unfair (in this case) and said in substance to the orderly when he insisted that he, the writer, should get excused, or go on guard, that he not only should do no such thing, and that there were not men enough in the regiment to put him on such duty. These were big words for a little man and private, too, to utter. But he uttered them all the same and is still alive and able to say that he did not "go to the major and did not get excused" nor did he go on extra duty, nor was he otherwise disturbed about it.

And here ends the writer's "Reminiscences" of the Bay Springs expedition out of which he got as much fun, fright and flagellations of one kind or another as any one in it, perhaps. And is satisfied with the way matters evened up.

[August 29, 1902]

CHAPTER FOUR

BETWEEN BATTLES

Plundering a Rebel Plantation

At the time the Bay Springs expedition heretofore mentioned in these "Reminiscences" came to Iuka on its return from Bay Springs, the military post of Iuka was under the command of Col. Miles of 27th Ill. Infy. But Gen. Mitchell, who had command of the expedition, and being of higher rank succeeded Miles in the command of the post upon his arrival.

It was generally reported in camp that Col. Miles had run matters, or rather had let matters run, at loose ends. So far, at least, as they concerned the citizen element, which was intensely disloyal. It was said that he even permitted citizens to utter treasonable and defiant language in and about his headquarters—without let or hindrance. Upon one occasion—the very day Mitchell's command arrived—two prominent and wealthy slavocrats met in front of his office and engaged in conversation concerning the disturbed condition of the country and the matter of taking the oath of allegiance to the government, as quite a number of citizens were at the time coming in and taking the oath.

One of these men asked the other if he intended to take the oath and he answered, "No, by, -------, I raised enough last year to support a band of guerrillas and have raised enough this year to support two, and I'll do it, too." Some one calling Miles' attention to the disloyal talk taking place, right under his eyes and ears, he simply stepped to the door and said to them that they had better stop such talk and get outside Federal lines or they might get into trouble. And they took his word and left. The name of one of these men was Mann, Richard Mann. And he resided just over the line in the State of Alabama, some 14 miles south of Iuka, which was near the line between the two States.

Gen. Mitchell, upon assuming the command of the post at Iuka, had been informed of Col. Miles' extreme leniency in dealing with the open disloyal and defiant citizens of the village and surrounding country, and as he had no great love or respect for southern "fire-eaters," [62] at best, having seen too much of their dastardly work in "bleeding Kansas" during the "border warfare" [63] from 1854 to 1860, to be overburdened even with common respect for them. And it is not, therefore, strange nor to be wondered at that he took prompt and decisive measures to change Miles' method of treating the enemy, and at the same time give an object lesson to them—show the power and ability of the government to enforce obedience to its mandates wherever its flag waved. And as a hint and strong reminder to Col. Miles of duties not well performed he determined to use him as one of his agents in bringing about the reform he deemed to be necessary. So on the evening of the day he succeeded to the command he sent for Miles and ordered him, so the camp news ran, to take five companies of his regiment and all the wagons and teams he could collect together and at midnight go to the plantation of one Richard Mann and bring him, his niggers and his cotton to Iuka and turn them over to the military authorities.

It was rumored in camp circles that Col. Miles took the fact of his selection for this important mission or, what comes nearer the truth, perhaps, raid, as indicating that Mitchell had been made aware of his (Miles') "glove handling" of Dick Mann and his confederates in treason, while in command of the post. And supposing his acts in this and other similar cases had brought him into disfavor with his superiors he determined to so execute the commission with which he was charged by Mitchell's order as to reinstate himself into favor. Be this as it may, it is certain that the order was carried out to the very letter, as the sequel given hereafter will amply show.

[July 21, 1902]

The very evening Miles received his orders to raid the Mann premises the writer's entire company was ordered to picket duty early the next morning, being Sunday, Aug. 10, 1862. The picket station assigned to the company was some two miles south of Iuka, and on the direct road leading from the village to the Mann plantation and the one that Miles' men and teams had passed over during the past night on their way to Mann's and would return on the same. So the writer witnessed the incidents he is about to relate in person, except those occurring at the Mann plantation which are from "hear say" evidence, and he believes substantially correct, as it is corroborated by the known results.

It is fact, however, that any old soldier will freely confess that much of the news passing in camp and elsewhere in an army received over the "grapevine" were anything but reliable, being generally the enunciation of the boys possessing optimistic proclivities and believes all is for the best and is happy and wants others to be so, so he starts a story in harmony with his feelings, "just for the fun of the thing," you know. Then the pessimist soldier, homesick and glum, who thinks everything is going to the bad, and from his diseased brain he sends out a report in consonance with his feelings. So the two classes of news go floating through the camp, believed by the few and hooted and jeered by the many. Such news the writer is not attempting to weave into the incidents related by him.

Miles arrived at his destination about day break and it being Sunday morning everything was still and quiet about the Mann mansion. Guards were thrown around it and some of the officers around the inmates and entered and as soon as the proprietor could arrange his toilet so as to be presentable, he entered the room occupied by the officers. It is not necessary to state that the old autocrat was for the once nonplussed—confounded—but nevertheless game. He was, perhaps, sixty, of portly build, hair tinged with gray and face smooth shaven, a fair type of the true southron who banked on his God given right to live by the sweat of some other men's brows, while he cracked the whip and laid on the lash. He was rich for this time and was married, but unfortunately childless within the realms of moral and civil laws. With the knowledge and consent of wife, he stepped outside of both these laws and became father to a son, whom he made his sole heir. And in the beautiful south land he was a gentleman all the same.

When the officers requested information as to where his cotton bales were stored or secreted his mouth closed as tightly as an oyster shell with a live oyster inside of it. After parleying with him for a time, without success, one of the officers drew a revolver and remarked, it was said, that just five minutes would be given in which to make answer to the question. He sulked to the very last moment and then directed his overseer, or slave driver as called in the north, who had just entered the room to show the officers the hiding place of the then [highly] valued cotton bales, fifty-three in number. He led them to a swamp not far distant, in the center of which the cotton was found with fagots easily ignited, placed in great abundance around it, ready to be fired whenever it should be necessary to prevent its falling into the hands of the hated Yankees. Fortunately for Uncle Sam, the Yanks had slipped up without giving warning of their approach and thus gave no opportunity for applying the match.

It was soon loaded on wagons and in due time found its way to Iuka and was turned over to the military powers for the use of the government, as the writer understood. He saw every bale of it when on the wagons and also on the platform ready for shipment.

Other articles that would go into the "support of a band of guerrillas" very nicely were found and like the cotton confiscated. Meat was discovered suspended in wells and in other unheard of places, which, with every other thing of use found on the premises, followed the trail of the cotton. But the writer would hazard too much in saying that these or any part of them were turned over to Uncle Sam. It would be safer to charge Col. Miles' boys with the theft, if any there was.

Mann possessed a huge old style coach or family "carry all," which in its day had no doubt been the envy of the surrounding plantations, far and near, and was still a useful article in a family. It was forced into service with a pair of mules attached, into which the owner, a prisoner under guard was thrust and with the balance of the stuff, taken to the "Headquarters of the army of Occupation," to Iuka, to abide its decrees.

But the better, and by far the more amusing part, from the writer's standpoint of view, is yet to come, as before stated his company, was doing picket duty along the road over which Miles' force passed in going to and returning from the Mann plantation at the time the return was made, so had a good opportunity of witnessing the somewhat of a non-descript procession or rather a series of processions, varying in kind and character from the sublime to the borders of the ridiculous.

Very soon after the arrival of the troops, with their teams and lumber wagons, at the Mann residence, the confusion they would of necessity create, aroused every darky on the plantation who came rushing in from his quarters to learn what was up at "Old Massa's" house, and seeing the "blue coats" and understanding their mission there, they evidently imagined that "Massa Lincum" or the day of judgment, or both together, had come, and that it meant no ill to them, whichever it was, so they regarded the disturbance in a far less serious light than did their old massa. And when they were told that if they wanted freedom, to strike out for Iuka their joy knew no bounds. "The year of Jubilee had come."[64] The goal of their fondest hopes and brightest visions was at last to be realized. This at least was the way the writer imagined the scenes around them, and the message imparted must have struck and impressed them. However this may be one thing is certain they waited for no second telling, but went, not standing on the order of their going thither. They were a motley lot, from coal black to saffron hue and of all ages, from the grandma of 80 to the picaninny at the breast.

They arrived at the picket post mentioned above between 8 and 9 o'clock in the morning. Several hours in advance of the troops and wagons, an old "granny," the oldest one among them in the lead, and as she came opposite the picket post Capt. Ford [65] in command, who, like the writer, was a "peculiar institution" said to her "Granny where are you going?" "Lausa massy sah, I doan know, but I hopes to freedom." He then asked how old she was and she replied, "Lordy massy I does not know," and turning around as to face the oncoming colored hosts— she being in the lead—she continued "does you see all dese? Dey is mosly all my chil'r'n, grand-chil'r'n and great grand-chil'r'n," and then "about faced" and trudged on toward Iuka and the land of "freedom" which she no doubt expected to reach soon.

[August 7, 1902]

If old granny was correct in claiming that the whole gang of darkies was 'mos'ly" all her descendants it would seem to demonstrate at least one redeeming trait in their master's character and that is that he kept his servants together—did not separate families—one of the most cruel and inhuman abuses of the unholy institution of slavery.

The writer never saw or heard of these "chattels" of Richard Mann again and therefore is not prepared to say whether or not freedom, which certainly came to them soon, bettered their condition. He can only hope it did.

About mid-day the troops and wagons of plunder, headed by Mann's "carry-all," with himself inside and two armed "blue coats" by his side, came along, making a very picturesque and not an easily described procession, and the writer will not, therefore, attempt further details more than to say Mr. Mann was placed under guard at Iuka, and shortly after attempting to break from his guard, who was a young stripling of a boy, but up to his duty all the same, he was shot in the leg, not seriously, however, but it stopped the attempted escape quick enough.

The writer having left Iuka shortly after the events here described occurred, cannot say what was finally done with him. But it is probable that he was discharged upon giving his parole.

[August 14, 1902]

The Consequences of Breaking Army Rules

While Gen. Jeff C. Davis's division was encamped on Cedar Creek, near Jacinto, Miss., in July, 1862, the writer's regiment, 25th Illinois, being a part of it, the writer was for the first and only time during his time of service as a soldier arrested for foraging on a small scale and on his own hook. Davis was a strict disciplinarian and his guards who were on the lookout for the "blue coats" who were in the habit of visiting orchards, cornfields, smokehouses, etc., without invitation from the owners [or] from Uncle Sam, and when they sighted a self appointed forager they generally took him in. They did the writer, anyhow, and this is the way it came to pass. The writer and big hearted Jerry Ishum, his comrade in arms, who was well known to the older citizens of Brushy Fork, tired of sow belly and beans diet day in and day out, and decided upon a change, a temporary one at least. With this end in view, they proceeded to get the necessary passes to enable them to get outside of camp lines. But they were only half successful, that is they obtained a pass for one only. However they made this one pass do double duty as will appear later on.

The first brigade of Davis' Division of which their regiment was a part, contained also at this time the 8th Kansas Infy., its members being typical Jay Hawkers who hated snakes. [See later correction] The brigade was enclosed by a chain of guards each regiment furnishing its quota of men for this duty, a deviation from the common mode, which was to let each regiment guard its own lines. Armed with the one pass, which Ishum held, and a "poke" or small bag, to hold the roasting ears, or any other "booty" they might find and appropriate to private use, which the writer carried, they set forth to find out how near two men could succeed in getting outside the brigade lines on one man's pass. They first approached the guards who were of their own regiment who said they would honor the pass, but could not recognize the "poke," as a pass. Defeated here, but by no means discouraged, they left, muttering as they went, "if at first you don't succeed, try, try again," and made for the Jayhawkers stationed on another part of the guard line. Their boys, many of whom had been in the "Border warfare" in "Bleeding Kansas" only a short time previous, were still harboring in their thoughts anything but good towards the slave holder and his unholy rebellion, and were ready and willing at any and all times to sanction, permit and do almost any injury to his person and property without remorse. And it is a fact the Kansas troops as a rule absolutely refused to guard the property of rebels suffering arrest and imprisonment for their refusal, oft times, as the writer can attest.

When the bearers of the "pass" and "poke" approached a Jayhawker sentinel, the first one they came to, Ishum presented his pass, which after a brief examination the sentinel returned to him saying, "It's all right" and turning to the writer he asked "and where is your pass?" "Here it is" the writer replied, flaunting almost in his face the poke "that is good enough," the guard replied, "pass out," and they at once crossed his "beat," and were beyond his authority for the time, and started anew for fresh fields of conflict and victory which also, came not as they would have had it.

The two foragers now having an open field for their exploits went first to Jacinto only a short distance from camp, and at this time the shire town of Tishomingo county, Miss. It was a sorrowful sight for a county seat town, the court house being perhaps twenty feet square and of two stories. But more need not be said here about this house, as the writer will have occasion to refer to it again, after he had learned to experience more of its details.

General Davis had his headquarters in the village, occupying a wood colored one story building at the east end of town, and was surrounded on three sides with peach trees full of ripe delicious fruitage, as the foragers discovered by a pretty thorough sampling, the general and his subordinates being absent. After sauntering around town for a while, and sampling peaches as noted above, and other fruits they left in search of something that would make a more substantial substitute for dry beans and sow belly than peaches and plums. They had noticed between camp and the village a field of corn just off the road a short distance which they had decided to investigate more closely when returning to camp. So turning their steps thitherward they were not long in reaching the village side of the field and were soon over the fence plucking and "poking" the nice pendant ears, in prime condition for the pot or for roasting. And by the time they had reached the opposite side of the field, which was not a large one, the "poke" carried by the writer was well filled.

[October 24, 1902]

(In the last installment of "Reminiscences," appearing in the INDEPENDENT of last week, the writer is made to say, by the omission of a part of a sentence in the copy, that the jayhawkers "hated snakes" a fact no doubt, but the writer did not say so, but he said that they "hated rebels worse than snakes hated Ireland, or other than St. Patrick hated snakes," which you see changes the hatred of the Jayhawkers from "snakes" to that of "rebels" and a completed sentence. A few other errors occurred that escaped the eye of the type setter and proof reader, which need not be pointed out as they were not material.)

They climbed upon the fence and sat awhile talking boastfully of their foraging exploits, and the pleasure anticipated from the substitution of roasting ears for navy beans, for a meal or two at least. But this pleasure like many other worldly ones, was short lived--nipped in the bud--and "died a born-in." Right under them lying in the shade of the fence upon which they were sitting two of Davis' Provost guards, listening to the vain gabble of the foragers, "counting their chickens before they were hatched," and holding their sides to keep from bursting with suppressed laughter. As they jumped from the fence to the ground unaware of the presence of either a friend or foe, and started for camp, the two guards sprang up, as by magic, and commanded them to halt, and they did, and at once realized with Bob Burns that "the best laid schemes of mice and men gang aft aglee." [66] It meant no roasting ears for supper. It meant, in fact was a complete collapse to all their visions of even a temporary change from army diet. Verily, "each pleasure has its poison, and every sweet a snare." But this mental moralizing, even if it really occurred, had no effect upon these provost guards. They were soldiers and a soldier's duty is to obey, and while they were marching their prisoners to the office of the provost marshall in the village, the writer will give a brief history of their captors, their company and regiment, first saying however, that he did not take with him the poke of green corn, for he had left the corn scattered over as large a space of the southern confederacy as he could make them cover by a vigorous sling of the sack he had filled with so much care, so did not appear in court as a material witness against him.

These guards belonged to the 59th Ill. Infy. originally the 9th Mo. Infy., [67] commanded by Col. P. Sidney Post, [68] a grand man, brilliant officer, and after the war a member of congress from this state, and died a few years ago while a member of that body.

Co. H of this regiment, was recruited largely from Coles and Edgar counties. Comrade Oliver Bell [69] of this city being one of them, and by the way friend Bell was doing guard duty over this same cornfield but in a different part of it at the time the writer and Ishum were taken in so slick, as noted above, and passing over the ground where the corn had been thrown by the writer just after the occurrence, he possessed himself of a few of the choicest ears, and feasted on the same that night while the writer languished "endurance vile," and in hunger as well. "One soweth and suffereth another reapeth and rejoiceth." [70] So it is, has, and ever will be.

[October 31, 1902]

In the article appearing in last week's INDEPENDENT the writer and his partner in the crime of taking without military orders, or the consent of the owner, a few roasting ears, which they did not get to eat, were left in charge of two provost guards who were conducting them to the provost marshall's office in Jacinto to be dealt with as that officer should determine after hearing the case, and the writer is here to say that the case went against them by a large majority, as they could not prove an "alibi" nor deny getting the corn. But they did not acknowledge the "corn" however. The provost order[ed] the prisoners to work upon the streets of the village, for which work they were furnished shovels. It was then near nightfall and their street labor lasted only a few minutes, when they were sent to the guard house, which was a room in the second story of the Tishomingo county court house, reference to which has heretofore been made by the writer. The room one of the jury rooms of the building, and was perhaps eight by ten feet square, without a chair, stool or anything else to sit upon save the bare floor which was well spread over with tobacco spit. In this room were when the "corn thieves" entered a jolly set of prisoners like themselves numbering some ten or twelve men, representatives from every regiment in the brigade, and all there, too, on the same charge—that of foraging—except the 8th Kansas boys, who were there because they refused to guard the property of those known to be in sympathy with the rebellion. There were two of the Jayhawkers in the gang, and they could have furnished music—chin music—for the entire house, if others had not contested with more or less succeess the attempted monopoly by them.

The writer has first and last, been mixed up, willingly and otherwise, with rowdy, rollicking crowds of them, of various shades of decency or rather of indecency, but that one surpassed them all, taken as a whole for unmentionable vulgarity, in speech and song, the jayhawkers in the lead. There was one feature of the entertainment that was really entertaining and thoroughly amusing and that was the part devoted to the relation, by the culprits, of the cause of their arrests. Some of these are still fresh in the mind of the writer, and he will attempt to give a few of them. One fellow a member of the 21st Ill. Inf. Grant's old regiment, by the name of Barnett, [71] a cousin of our Geo. D Barnett, had in some manner got outside the guard lines with his gun, and proceeded to find something to shoot at that would make a substitute for some of the worn out articles of army diet, "bacon and beans" for instance. And in his search he came upon a flock of sheep and opened fire upon it and brought down a fine fat wether, and brought upon himself some of Davis' provost guards before the sheep was done kicking, so the guards got it and Barnett got arrested and a night, at least in a room in what is supposed to be a "temple of justice," a courthouse, but in this case a "bastille" after the old Spanish and French order.

Discipline in the army is of the utmost importance and punishment for any infraction of orders along this line, is eminently proper, but the punishment should not consist in whole or in part of crowding together in a small, illy ventilated and filthy room, such an one as the writer has attempted to describe here.

Another "prisoner" was fond of chicken and in attempting to satisfy this fondness, he endeavored in broad day light to run down a spring chicken, and was himself run down and before he got even a tail hold on the pullet, by the same omnipresent guards. But in this case it is some satisfaction to know that the guards did not get the pullet, unless they returned after nightfall and took her from the roost.

Another "boy" had an experience something like this; he got so tired of the bacon Uncle Sam furnished, and longed so intensely for the home made kind, that he finally "slipped guards," and got on the outside of the guard lines, and into a smoke house, and then turned up at, and in the guard house to keep the company of the writer and Ishum, leaving his ham with the "scouting guards" to compensate them for the trouble of running him in.

[November 7, 1902]

And so the tales ran, interspersed with doggerels that will not bear repeating here, until well along in the night, when it was suggested by the writer who had illy enjoyed the carnival of smut and shame, that it was time to "turn in" and turn out the lights—only in this case however, and that a poor article of "tallow dip." This suggestion was by degrees agreed to and then the real fun began, as attempting to spread twelve men in horizontal position, over a space too small for ten men to thus occupy, without putting one man on top of another, several experiments were resorted to and each was a sad failure. The space would not expand, nor would the men "contract." So they could choose between an upright position, with liberty of action, and an horizontal one and be sandwiched between two comrades and squeezed out of shape. They all finally came to the horizontal attitude, not to sleep for that was not possible, but the better to growl and swear, and they made the foul air fairly blue with these, and thus the night dragged its weary length along, until the sun dawned to the delight of twelve weary and abused defenders of the flag, not in their arrest but in their confinement in an overcrowded and filthy room, which they had no military or moral right to force upon them, as a punishment for disobedience of order. But the "roasting" ear culprits survived the night of "mirth and misery," [72] and in the early morn after a breakfast on a par with their slumber had been doled out to them, they were put on the streets again with shovels, like paddies on a railroad. But the work, like the evening before, was cut short, not by the curtains of night however, but by other influences, quite as potent it seemed. For Capt. Chas. A Clark, [73] of their regiment came riding by, and seeing the writer, whom he well knew, in this unmilitary sort of exercise, inquired into the cause, and learning the facts, went direct to the provost's office, but what occurred there the writer never knew, but he knows that very soon after this they were sent for by the provost who giving them a mild lecture on army discipline discharged and sent them rejoicing to their regiment, which upon reaching they were hailed with boisterous shouts of "green corn, green corn," a name that stuck to them for several days when something newer turned up in the company and their exploits were forgotten and they had rest. This was the first and last experience of the writer with provost guards and guard houses, and it was all sufficient too.

[November 14, 1902]

Nearly Captured by Rebel Rangers

The writer will now attempt before leaving Iuka, at and near which so many incidents in his short soldier life occurred, to relate how near he came of being gobbled up by a roving band of Roddy's partisan rangers. A few days after the events just mentioned, he was ordered to take from Corinth to Iuka a lot of bread in the loaf, barreled up, for the use of the hospital and the troops stationed there. At the time of which we are speaking, military trains were running on the old Charleston & Memphis R. R. between Corinth and Florence, Alabama, passing through Iuka, and the bread was to go by rail. The bread was packed in barrels, the barrels placed on the platform and the train men ordered to put them on the cars, the train being then on the track ready to pull out. The writer then sauntered about the train, awaiting it's departure. In a very few moments the roaring whistle sounded and the train began to move. Just as the writer was in the act of getting aboard he noticed his bread was still on the platform and the train was in motion. Not caring to go without taking his baggage he did not board the train and it pulled out, leaving him and the loaves behind. And it turned out to be a fortunate "leaving" once at least in his life, for when the train reached the vicinity of Burnsville, about midway between Corinth and Iuka, it was captured and burned [74] by a gang of Roddy's ragamuffin rangers, who had torn up the track for a short distance and then laid in wait for the train.

There was not much booty and but few men on the train. The first was appropriated and the other paroled. The prowling rangers did not tarry long after firing the cars for the woods were full of Yankee cavalry, of which Roddy had a wholesome dread. The track was but little damaged and was soon repaired and the following afternoon the writer got his barrels of bread aboard a train and delivered them safely to Iuka.

The train stopped at the place where the wreck of the previous day had occurred and the scene again brought to mind Sherman's definition of war and the writer was glad the Rebs did not get a chance to give him a taste of Sheol the day before.

[October 3, 1902]

The "Accommodating" Dr. Simmons

While in the provost marshal's office at Iuka, in August, 1862, the writer became well acquainted with a somewhat noted doctor by the name of Simmons, who was the son of the proprietor of the once famous and still popular remedy known as "Simmons' Liver Invigorator," once advertised as extensively in the public press as Royal Baking Powder now is. The younger Simmons, the older one being dead, had succeeded his father in the manufacturing of the "Invigorator" and was at this time engaged in this business. He had his own press and printing outfit and printed the various labels, circulars and other printed matter used in the preparation of the medicine for the market. He was, as was father before him, a minister in the M. E. church, South, [75] but not in the regular work. He seemed to be a fair minded man, but somewhat on the "policy order," [76] which no doubt he thought stood him in hand to be, for Iuka was sometimes in the possession of one and sometimes in the possession of the other army. So he stood in an "accommodating" attitude and could "run with the hare and bark with the hound" [77] if need be.

The writer put the doctor's loyalty and temper, too, to the test one day and while he did not succeed in his object, he held the right of way all the same. And this is the way it happened. The office had run short of a certain blank and the writer concluded he could save Uncle Sam the expense of buying these by utilizing Dr. Simmon's printing outfit and running them off himself. 'Tis true he had never seen a printing press in operation a half dozen times in his life nor had he any more conception of the printer's art in any of its details than the average frequenters of our cold storages [78] have of common decency and the sanctity of the oath. And yet he supposed he could set up and run off these simple blanks in a jiffy "all by himself alone." So elated with this thought and the further thought of saving the government a few pennies he called on the doctor and informed him of the object of his visit and his desire to proceed to business without further unnecessary delay. The doctor seemed a little frustrated at the situation, but finally asked, in a demure tone of voice, "Did you ever operate a printing press?" And this question, in turn, frustrated the writer and set him back several points, but answered with a little quaver in his voice, "No, not as a profession. But he has seen them operated a few times and he thinks it will be no trick to run one."

This reply, judged by looks and acts, was not very convincing, but believing the U. S. government was in some sense behind it, he bottled his wrath and swallowed his disgust, but ventured to mildly hint that he himself knew nothing about the practical workings of the press, which was as much as to say to the writer that he would get no assistance from him.

All this had occurred outside of the printing office, so the writer suggested that they go into the office and examine the concern and see how intricate it was. And he led the way, not for love, but for policy's sake, mixed with fear of offending Uncle Sam, possibly. Now, as has been before intimated and as the reader will also discover from the language he uses here, that what he did not then, and what he does not now know, about the art of printing would make a book of unwieldy size. The press was an ordinary hand concern, such as were in use forty years ago, and was used only for printing the various forms of patent medicine advertising. Upon a table was one of these advertisements in "form," that is, the type had been set and placed in form and held in place by means of strips of lath of the proper length and size inserted between the walls of the "form" and the type, and pressed securely against the type by little wedges or keys driven between the walls and the strips, thus keeping them in place, as "set," until they were transferred to the press. If this description does not corroborate what he said about his knowledge of the printing business, the writer has mistaken the intelligence of the readers of the INDEPENDENT, that's all. The result of the investigation of the printing press, the writer is forced to confess was disastrous to his boasted ability to be able to manipulate one. For in his attempt to ascertain how the type was held in the "form" he knocked the thing into "pi," [79] and he was not over two-thirds of a minute in doing either. Of course this act did not increase, to any great extent, the doctor's love for the hated Yankees, and the government had to buy the blanks after all, that the writer had intended to furnish it free gratis. "Sic transit gloria mundi." [80] He hopes the old press has been superseded by an improved up-to-date one and that the doctor is still engaged in patching up the livers of the people with "Simmon's Liver Invigorator."

The writer called on the doctor once after this printing office "picnic," when he knocked types into "pi," just after the battle of Iuka, and he took great interest in showing the writer a cave he had dug in the side of a bank near his premises in which he and his household had taken shelter from shot and shell at the battle a few days before. And it answered the purpose, to perfection, too. There was a regiment of Mississippi troops encamped near his residence at the time the battle commenced, which was hurriedly ordered to the front and as it was without tents, the boys packed, or rather piled up, their knapsacks and their meager supply of camp equipage on their camp grounds and hastened to the contest raging a mile or two to the south. And they were all so disabled, so the doctor stated, in the fight, or had left the field as hurriedly as they had their camp and so they could not return for traps and it fell into the hands of the "blue coats," which proved to be a "booty" without "beauty" or benefit.

The doctor, although a preacher, was a slave holder and had one argument, at least, in favor of the perpetuity of the peculiar institution, that was simple and unique, if not convincing to an outsider. It runs like this: "You know," said he, addressing the writer, "that many of the best citizens of the south, even of the better class, were nursed (some times even at the breast) and cared for when young by slave women to whom they became much attached, so the old 'mammas' on the plantation who have helped raise their master's families are usually held in esteem by masters and children. Why, don't you know," he continued, warming up to his subject, "that I think as much of going to see my slave mamma as I do of visiting my own mother and if slavery is abolished," he went on to say, "these 'mammas' may leave their masters and become lost to us."

This was an argument, a weighty one indeed—in his own mind. He would hold three millions of human beings in bondage, because there were a few thousands among them, perhaps, who were held in some sort of esteem, and who might wander out of sight and hearing of the few who might esteem them. For it is a fact, though not generally known, that 300,000 men owned more than four-fifths of the 3,000,000 slaves held in the south at the time of its attempted secession from the union in 1861. These 300,000 men dominated the south, formulated its laws and led the masses, who had no grievances to complain of, into war, which if it had have been successful would only have worsened their social and financial conditions, so blinded do men sometimes become to their own interests and see it not until the mischief is done, when it is too late.

CHAPTER FIVE

THE BATTLES OF IUKA AND CORINTH

The Battle of Iuka

Shortly after the events related in the writer's last article of "Reminiscences" of the War of 1861-65 the Union forces were all withdrawn from Iuka except a small body of cavalry left there to guard a small quantity of army stores, mostly flour, which were very soon after captured by the enemy's cavalry which dashed upon our troopers "all of a sudden" and took the whole outfit [81] and held the place until after the battle of Iuka, which was fought on the evening of September 19, 1862.

A force of Confederates under Gen. Sterling Price on its way, it is supposed, to join Bragg in his invasion of Kentucky, culminating in the battle of Perryville, Oct. 8, 1862, had encamped in and a little south of Iuka.

To prevent this juncture with Bragg and if possible destroy or at least seriously cripple Price's army Gen. Rosecrans sent three divisions of his forces in and around Corinth, amounting to some eight or nine thousand men. The division commanders were Gens. Ord, Stanley and Hamilton. And they took parallel roads, Ord on the north, Stanley the center and Hamilton the south. Rosecrans planned the order of march, selected the camping place for each division and the time and manner of the attack. According to this plan, Hamilton who took the south road, was to go into camp on the evening of Sept. 19th at a small stream just south of Iuka and near Barnett's cross roads. The other divisions were to camp in supporting distances of each other and to Hamilton's as well.

But Hamilton in getting the position assigned him found it in the possession of the enemy and in his effort to dislodge him, brought on a general engagement and the battle of Iuka was fought on the evening of the 19th September 1862, and not on the 20th, as arranged by Rosecrans, the brunt of it being borne by Hamilton's division. A part of Stanley's forces came upon the field just at the close of the battle. It may be said, however, that it was from no fault of Stanley and Ord that they failed to support Hamilton. The battle was precipitated and unexpectedly, even to Hamilton himself, brought on and fought before Stanley and Ord could get upon the field. The battle was hotly contested and both sides suffered heavily. [82] And when darkness had caused a cessation of the conflict it was supposed by the Federals, at least, that it would be renewed in the morning. But during the night Price left the field with his shattered forces in such haste and disorder that much of their camp equipage and many a poor fellow's knapsack were left behind. And they got such a good start on the Yanks that they could not overtake them. But they retreated to the south and not toward Bragg's army, to the north. So Rosecrans' object was accomplished so far at least as the prevention of the union of Price's and Bragg's forces was concerned. [83]

The writer will attempt to relate a few incidents connected with this battle, not, however, from personal observation, for he was not in the engagement. But he was at Gen. Rosecrans' headquarters, as a clerk, at the time and had therefore good opportunities for getting the particulars concerning the battle. And a few days after the fight he was sent to Iuka to parole quite a number of Confederate soldiers who were sick and could not go with their commands when they retreated and were captured and held as prisoners by the Yanks. So he had some personal relations with the immediate results of the battle which he may refer to later on.

During the hottest part of the engagement, and it was hot enough from start to finish, the 17th Iowa Reg. which happened to be in front of the 39th Ohio Infy. though their relative positions were not known to each other, became demoralized from some cause and fell back in confusion, running into, over and through the Ohio regiment, which was or just had been lying down, throwing it into disorder but not into a panic.

One writer states in the columns of the *National Tribune* that the Ohio boys mistook the Iowans for rebels and fired into them. The writer thinks this is a mistake. There was no doubt great confusion, and the Iowa boys were completely panic stricken, too much to have done any serious harm with their fire arms. And the Ohio troops did not have time to use theirs, and even if they had had the time their firing, in the darkness, would have been as dangerous to their own men as it would have been to the Hawkeyes or the enemy, so they would not have been likely to do so reckless a job.

Gen. Rosecrans, in his order congratulating the troops on their valor and victory at Iuka, took occasion to say that he was sorry to be under the necessity of excepting from these congratulations the 17th Iowa Infy. whose conduct in action had brought a stain upon the fair name of the American soldiery and he hoped it would embrace the first opportunity to wipe out the stain from its records. And it did so.

[August 14, 1902]

Just two weeks later it did cover itself with glory, washing out the stain with the blood of many of its brave boys at the battle of Corinth, Oct. 4, 1862, [84] an allusion to which may again be made.

John W. Cook, of this city, was a member of the 39th Ohio and was in the battle of Iuka, as was also a brother of the writer. Comrade Cook was lying down hugging his gun when the Iowa boys stampeded and ran into his regiment, as stated above, when a frightened Hawkeye, in his run to the rear, got his foot tangled up somehow with Cook's gunstrap and jerked the gun from his embrace, leaving our patent attorney armless for the time. He can tell you much more graphically than can the writer the difficulty he had in the darkness of finding his arms again, a weapon very important to a soldier on the battlefield. But he found and no doubt used to good purpose his firearms.

Paroling Captured Confederates

[O]ne result of the battle of Iuka was the leaving on our hands at the time the enemy retreated quite a number of sick men, some 150 or more all told. And the writer who was at the time on detached service at Gen. Rosecrans' headquarters at Corinth was sent to Iuka to parole such of them as desired to give their paroles. He arrived at Iuka just at night fall and proceeded at once to fulfill his mission. A church building belonging to the M. E. Church, south, had been converted into a hospital, if bare walls and bare floors can be called one. The seats had been removed and the poor inmates, every one of them too feeble to sit up, were laid in parallel rows reaching the whole length of the building, and between aisles lying with their feet together, some having blankets under them, others nothing at all but the poorest kind of makeshift clothing. But the most of the poor fellows had some sort of an improvised pillow for their heads. They presented a sad picture indeed. A few tallow candles placed in different parts of the house gave a feeble, sombre light which, reflecting upon the upturned wan, bloodless and cadaverous faces of many who had been lured from home by designing men to engage in a struggle, the success of which meant the degradation of the "poor white trash" among whom many of them were classed, no doubt, by those whose false and deceptive arguments were the causes that placed them in this condition.

The process of paroling was very simple, the blanks being all filled out and ready for signing except dating, consequently all there was to do was to explain when requested the significance of the paper and get the signatures of the unfortunate and misguided men. The main trouble was in getting their names subscribed to the parole blank, as not one in ten could write his own name. A greater per cent. might have done so had they been in health. But as it was the writer had to write the names and then place the pen in the nerveless fingers and guide the feeble hand to the proper place and assist it in making the "sign manuel," which was generally in this X form.

Many of them had no conception of the word "parole" and when told that it was simply, in this case, a promise not to engage in the war against the government until they should be exchanged in usual form, it did not seem to impress them at all favorably, as they apparently took it to mean going back on the southern confederacy. But when they were informed that by giving their parole or promise they might be allowed by their government furloughs to go home and remain until they were exchanged, they gladly consented, and every man in the building gave his written parole. But the writer is quite certain that not all by far of these poor fellows ever received furloughs to visit their earthly homes for in his opinion some of them took their everlasting furlough before the setting of another sun. One poor fellow, he is quite sure, never saw another sunrise, for the clammy sweat on hand and face, with the ominous rattle in throat, indicated unmistakably that he was in the very "hour and article of death," when he subscribed, with the writer's assistance, his name on his written parole. This hospital scene gives emphasis to the declaration made by the old war trained hero, Gen. Wm. Tecumseh Sherman, that "war is hell."

It was quite late when his work was completed at the church and you may imagine that he was glad to get away from the horrible scenes he was compelled to witness there.

[August 21, 1902]

The next morning hearing that there was a Confederate officer being cared for at a private house in the village he started on a search for the place and soon found it. And was admitted into the presence of the officer, who proved to be a captain and belonged to a Texas regiment. He occupied the best room and bed in the house and presented a marked contrast with the boys in the old church house. He had so far convalesced to be able to sit up in bed.

When the writer informed him the nature of his business, he asked to see one of the parole blanks, which having read he handed back, saying, "If you will erase the 'so-called' in it I will sign it." The "so-called" he objected to was placed before the words "Confederate States" in the blanks. It will be remembered that Uncle Sam did not recognize the Southern Confederacy as a nation but as States in rebellion, so when using the name assumed by the States in rebellion, which was "Confederate States of America"; the government invariably prefixed the words "so-called" to the words "Confederate States" in all its communication and official business with the so-called Confederate States.

The writer informed the objecting "so-called" captain, with emphasis, that there would be no erasures made, that if he gave his parole it would be given exactly as written in the blank he had just read and not otherwise. He replied, "I can't give it." "Very well," said the writer, "my business is done with you," and started toward the door. He stopped him, saying, "You won't change it, then?" and was answered as before. He then said or rather muttered as if talking to himself, "It does seem a little hard to remain here a prisoner when I could perhaps, if paroled, go home and stay until exchanged." To which an encouraging nod was given by the writer, and at the same time offered him back the blank, which taking he sat up in the bed and drawing up his legs to form a rude table and placing the blank thereon, signed it in a nice smooth hand. And upon being complimented for his penmanship he observed that he had been a school teacher for years. And by the way, it is the writer's impression of the 150 or more who gave paroles his was the only name written in a legible hand.

What disposition was made with these men or any part of them the writer never knew. Doubtless, those surviving were in time exchanged, but where the poor fellows spent the interim between the giving of their paroles and their exchange he is left to his own surmisings. He hopes they all got the coveted furlough and spent the time pleasantly with their mothers, sisters, aunts and sweethearts. But he cannot say that such were his hopes when he suggested to them the "furlough consideration" as an incentive for them to give their paroles. Forty years have materially weakened the asperities engendered by the war, and he feels differently toward the boys who wore the gray to what he did when he was wearing the blue. But he still is of the opinion that the more the prime movers in that unholy rebellion received of what old grizzly Sherman designated war as being hell, the better. For they knowingly and purposely engaged in waging war in the interest of human slavery, which ever tends to bring cheap labor into direct competition with the labor of the freeman. But it is well, it is in fact better, to remember that the war with all its asperities, its hell, is happily long since over and that we are brothers now.

[August 28, 1902]

The Battle of Corinth

The Battle of Corinth—sometimes called the second battle—the siege of Corinth being the first—was one of the important battles of the war of the rebellion, and was fought on 3rd and 4th of October, 1862. The Confederates were led by Gens. Price and Van Dorn, Gen. Rosecrans commanding the Federal forces.

The writer was present, not as a participant on the bloody field however, but as an attache of the commissary department which gave him a favorable opportunity for witnessing the battle, and of hearing direct from the field, in every part of it, every few minutes.

Before entering into the particulars of this battle, let the writer go back a few days and relate some facts in his personal history showing how he came to be at Corinth, at this time when his regiment was in Kentucky. He has mentioned the fact more than once in these reminiscent articles that he had been detached from his company and regiment, by an order of Gen. Rosecrans and assigned to other duty, and he was serving in this relation when his regiment was ordered back to Kentucky, which, with the fact that at this time he was disabled in his feet by poison, account for his remaining behind. About the middle of Sept., some three weeks before the battle, he entered the office of Capt. Miles the provost marshal at Rosecrans' headquarters, some five miles south of Corinth, as clerk. But a few days later he was taken sick, which cut his labors short in this office. He was taken sick in the night, and he well remembers, that "old Rosey" as the boys loved to call him, came into the tent—which was also the office—in the morning, and seeing some one in the "bunk," and not knowing who it was nor the condition of the occupant, he asked Capt. Miles "what in h—l this man was doing in bed at this time of day?" The Capt. replied that it was one of his clerks and he was sick. "O, indeed" said "Old Rosey," "is that so," and approaching the couch of the clerk, he spoke kindly to him, expressing a wish for his speedy recovery. "Rosey" was a good Catholic, and an expert in the use of cuss words as well. He usually had a Priest at his headquarters, who was made to answer a good purpose quite often. Father Stacy, a good and loyal man was at his headquarters at this time. The writer heard him once take a rebel deserter through the "sweat mill" as thoroughly as the most expert Pinkerton detective could a "suspect." He pumped the Johnny dry in short order getting all the poor fellow knew or could tell as to the number and location of the forces he had just left, whether or not the information was of benefit to us, the writer does not know. He knows that the Priest knew just how to get hold of the reb to get all that was within him out. Gens. Rosecrans and Stanley, seem to have been chums, as they were often together, which reminds the writer of the following little incident that occurred in his presence once. It was at the R. R. depot at Iuka, Miss., at a time when there was an order in force prohibiting soldiers from loitering or lounging around places where their duties did not require them to be. A sergeant from an Ohio regiment that had been ordered to move to some other point, was sitting in the shade of the station house, when Rosecrans and Stanley came along, and stopped opposite the sergeant. Stanley asked the "Buckeye" sergeant where he belonged and the sergeant told him his company and regiment. The general then asked where his regiment was, and was informed by the sergeant, in a gentlemanly manner. He was then asked where his command was going? The sergeant before replying hesitated and eyed the two major generals rather closely and then gave the information fully. It may just here be stated that both these officers wore long linen dusters over their "uniform" coats, so there was nothing in sight on their clothing to indicate their rank, and the sergeant had no doubt discovered this fact, if indeed he knew, or suspected them of being officers. Be this as it may when Stanley asked him what he was doing there, the sergeant at once retorted: "It's none of your d-m-d business." "Stop, stop," said the general waving his hand toward the sergeant who had remained sitting, "remember you are talking to Gen. Rosecrans." "O," replied the sergeant: "excuse me, I did not know I had the honor of talking with Gen. Rosecrans." And the "tit for tat" ended here, with the lone buckeye in the saddle, and the Gen. unhorsed even if he did assume "old Rosey's" name. Both generals left with a broad grin on their faces, leaving the sergeant with a broader one lighting up his visage.

But resuming. The writer was too sick to long remain without medical attention. So he and his outfit were put in an ambulance, and started for some one of the many hospitals in and around Corinth. But the clerk, sick as he was, did not like the idea of being dumped into any hospital. He had seen enough of them to create in his mind, an abhorrence of the whole hospital business. And as he had a little money and fair outfit of clothing and blankets, he told the driver to take him to commissary department, at Corinth, then in charge of Capt. Ferry, a cousin of U. S. Senator Ferry, of Michigan, and relative of the great Seedman D. M. Ferry, with whom he was acquainted, and this is how it came about that the writer was at Corinth during the great battle there, on October 3rd and 4th, 1862. He had so far recovered from his sickness when the battle came off that he could assist in the office work.

It will be remembered by those familiar with the details of the battle of Corinth, that it began at Chewalla, some eight or ten miles west of Corinth. Gen. Oglesby-- "our own Uncle Dick" [85] —occupied this outpost with his division, and he was attacked on Oct. 1 [3rd], by a largely superior force and gradually forced back upon Corinth, getting within the protection of its defense on the evening of Friday, the 3rd. In the Friday fighting, Gen. Oglesby was quite severely wounded, [86] and his division suffered, more or less in killed and wounded. [87]

The general plan of the battle on the 2nd day, was Hamilton's division on our extreme right, to his left and a little to the south, Stanley's division; in Stanley's front and to westward Davis's division. West of the Mobile and Ohio R. R. and south of the Memphis and Charleston R. R. McKean's division, and between McKean's division and Davis's the Ohio Brigade was located with Fort Robinett in its front, and the Memphis and Charleston R. R. on its left. In this brigade was the 39th Ohio reg. of which Comrade J. W. Cook of this city, and a brother of the writer, of Melrose,

Ia., were members. The former can, if he will, tell you something about the canteens, jugs, bottles and pails of whiskey that found their way into his regiment one night during the engagement, and their effect upon the boys, all of which canteens &c. &c. were filled by the writer from barrels of the stuff stored in the commissary building, and many of like vessels were also filled by him and taken to other commands on the bloody field. But the writer did not do this kind of work "of his own free will and accord." He was ordered by his superior to do it, and you know the first thing a soldier learns is that he "has no will of his own." His duty is to obey.

The writer will never forget the work he performed during those two days of blood and carnage. It consisted in its entirety of drawing and filling the vessels that came in from every part of the field. It should be remembered that whiskey was issued to officers only, who carried commissions. The government never sold whiskey in any form to non-commissioned officers or privates, and it would wipe out a long standing disgrace, if it would stop the sale of the crime producing stuff, to officers, and cashier every one of them who used it.

A few incidents of interest to the writer, at least, of the great battles with some of the results will follow.

[January 1, 1903]

The position of our forces on the morning of the second day of the battle of Corinth was given in the writer's last article, which was practically Hamilton's division on the right, Davis the center, and McKean on the left, with the Ohio brigade sandwiched between McKean and Davis.

The Confederates, under Van Dorn, approached from the right, Price coming in from the left. Quoting from the language of another, [88] "The assault was begun by an impetuous charge by the latter general (Van Dorn). Little was done, however, the first day." It may be here stated that while it was true there was no decisive results in the first day's fighting, and yet it is equally true that there was much severe fighting and skirmishing during the day, in one of which the three times governor of the great state of Illinois and once one of its representatives in the United States Senate, Richard J. Oglesby, our own "Uncle Dick" was seriously wounded.

But continuing the quotation, "Early October 4th Price's column advanced, drawn up like a wedge. The charge was a daring one, but the Confederates were driven back and literally cut to pieces. [89] The Texas and Mississippi troops under Rodgers [90] fared as badly. They fled in disorder and were pursued for some distance by an Ohio regiment." This in a nut-shell gives the results of the sanguinary and decisive battle.[91] At its close there laid scattered over the bloody field 315 Federal and 1565 Confederate soldiers cold in death, besides the wounded, which are always more numerous than the killed. It will be observed that the enemy's loss in killed was five times greater than our own.[92] The writer will never as long as his mental facilities, small as they may be, shall perform these functions sanely, forget the scenes and incidents he, there and then witnessed. The incessant roar of cannon, the rattle of musketry, the shouts of the soldiers running hither and thither, of aides and orderlies, the wild and excited movements of citizens and the coming in from the front of the faint-hearted and weak-kneed stragglers and their gathering into little knots after getting into places of supposed safety. All come up before the mind and vision of the writer to-day as vividly as they did forty years ago when they actually transpired in his presence. No indeed! Time can efface them from memory never!

Now, with the reader's indulgence, the writer will as briefly as may be done, consistent with the facts, attempt to relate some of the incidents, personal and otherwise, witnessed by him during those two days of awful blood and carnage, without regard to the order of their occurrence, however. During the last charge, as bold and impetuous as it was disastrous to the chargers, made by the enemy on the last day of the great battle, when it seemed probable that they might break through our lines and enter the town (in fact, a few "Johnnies" did actually succeed in some way in getting through and were killed within a few yards of Gen. Rosecrans' headquarters tents that stood near the northwest corner of the public square. [93] However, if there had been no such danger the fact that the enemy had approached so near the town, having got east of the Mobile & Ohio railroad, that the shots from their musketry even endangered the lives and safety of citizens and other non-combatants. So under these conditions old Rosey ordered all non-combatants to move to the east a short distance to where a depression in the landscape afforded protection, and there was a general rush to this place by the excited populace. And the writer went also in obedience to orders. And it was while he was on the way to this retreat that the cannon ball went crashing through the Tishomingo hotel and killed a soldier that was being carried on a stretcher, which incident has been often noticed in the public print [94] and also in history. He cannot say that he saw that identical ball, but he will say that on this occasion he came near seeing one on its passage through space as it is possible for one to be thus seen. He saw the "blue streak" it makes at least he has ever since believed he saw it. And he absolutely knows that he heard it cutting the air in its mad flight.

Near the place, where the non-combatants rendezvoused a new fort was being built, the guns, large siege ones, were already in place. The enemy was pressing us so stubbornly that orders were given to turn these 32 pounders upon them, the guns elevated so as to throw the balls over the houses and the heads of our own men. There was several darkies—"contrabands" they were then called—at work on the fort which was built somewhat below the surface of the ground, and were not apprised of the order to use the guns, so when they discharged the darkies were taken so completely by surprise when the awful report that rent the very heavens came that it would have brought a smile to the face of an iceberg to have seen them tumbling over each other in their mad efforts to get out of the pit and away from the guns. And they "got," too. This incident occurred, just as the writer was passing the fort on his way to the "retreat" from rebel balls. He found the shelter, but remained there only a short time. For soon shouts, vigorous and loud, came wafted on the breezes from our boys at the front, presaging a victory either temporary or permanent. And the writer did not wait to learn which it was. He at once started on the "quick step," in company with a citizen clerk in the commissary department, from the Hawkeye state, for the source of the shouting, and stopped not until the bloody field was reached. And the awful scenes of the hotly contested battle lay before him, in all of its fullness and gory hideousness. The angry contestants had separated and the clash of arms had ceased and the ground over which the two surging armies so stubbornly had contested for the mastery was left to the dead, the dying and the disabled of both, with "Old Glory" waving in triumph in the evening breezes. The shouting and cheering that had reached the ears of the writer and others in their temporary retreat was caused or hastened, it was said, by the presence on the field immediately following the repulse of the enemy of "Old Rosey," who said to his powder-stained blue coats, "Boys, you

Daniel O. Root

have done nobly; you have thrashed the enemy and driven them back. But they are just over there in the woods trying to reform their depleted ranks, and if they return you will double the dose, won't you?" And the answer was the shouts and cheers above mentioned, which hearing the enemy, supposing it to be caused by the arrival of reinforcements, which was expected from Jackson, Tenn., was thrown into the utmost confusion and disorder, bending and breaking their swords and muskets by striking them against tree logs and fences and casting them away to lighten their burdens and aid their escape from the victorious Yankees. These bent and broken arms were brought into Corinth by the wagon loads and would have formed a museum of war weapons of the non-descript order that would defy all competition in its line. The "Johnnies" could do a very creditable job of fighting with very indifferent arms, judging from the appearance of those brought in, as noted above.

Other incidents will follow.

[January 23, 1903]

The writer promised to give in this communication a resume of the incidents witnessed by him at and during the great battle of Corinth, October 3rd and 4th, 1862. And he will now proceed to fill this promise. When the writer arrived on the battlefield, which was very soon after the fighting had ceased, as noted in his last article, Gens. Rosecrans and Stanley were both passing over the field, mounted and together, as they often were, viewing the dead. They were in that part of the field in front of Hamilton's division, where the ground was literally covered with the dead, largely of the enemy's, too. Among those who had fought their last battle, was a Col. Johnson, who was commanding a rebel brigade when shot. He was a large portly man, dressed in a short, tight fitting coat, black, a vest and pants of same material, with silk socks or stockings, in fact his dress throughout was far superior to the most of the officers of his rank in the Confederate service, even at this date. Around the dead officers were gathered several sight-seers when the two generals, Rosecrans and Stanley, came riding by and seeing the group of men the writer being one, halted and ordered, or rather requested, the men to stand aside a little so they could see without dismounting. And after reviewing the remains for a time Stanley said to "Old Rosey": "General, did you ever see him before?" "Yes," replied the general, "once, only, at Fort Smith, several years ago, he then being a Captain in the U. S. A." Johnson like many other officers in the regular army who had received military training at the nation's expense, turned traitor to his country by entering the army of the so-called confederate states, and gave his life for the lost cause.

In connection with this incident, let the writer go a little further into the details by drawing upon his imagination for material. Not far from where Col. Johnson fell, the 64th Illinois, [95] a regiment of sharp shooters, was stationed, a large oak tree had been fallen and the brush and smaller limbs removed, behind which the sharp shooters had taken shelter during the battle, and were in a good and safe position to "pick off" with their trusty long rifles, the enemy's officers. Now behind this fallen tree, lay one of these boys, cold in death, with a bullet hole through his head, the ball entering the forehead right between the eyes, with his death grip still on his gun. The rebel colonel had met his fate, and "bit the dust" within fair range of the sharp shooter's rifle, and not to exceed one hundred yards from his station, and the ball that had accomplished its deadly mission struck in identically the same place as that received by the sharp shooter. Now would it be much of a strain upon the imagination to draw the inference that the ball from the sharp shooter's rifle had laid low the Col., and then a random shot from some "gray coat's" musket had retaliated, so to speak and sent the soul of the "blue coat" to accompany the spirit of the Col. to a land where wars come not; the writer thinks not.

One of the most pathetic sights that ever come to the eye of the soldier who is familiar with sad sights the writer witnessed in the near vicinity of the incidents just related. It still haunts, quite oft, the day time dreams of the relator and emphasizes the terrors of the war, and furnishes a sound reason why differences between nations should be adjusted by peaceful ambition and not the arbitrament of war. Under a large oak tree, with his head resting on one of its rough ragged roots, placed there no doubt by a comrade, was lying a confederate soldier in all the agony and contortions of death, when the writer and a citizen clerk from Iowa, whose name cannot now be recalled, approached him just after hostilities had ceased, on the last day's fight. He was literally shot to pieces, and so bloody an object as it is possible to conceive of. The awful contortion of his arms, the only part of his body that he seemingly could use had carried and spread his life's blood over every part of the body and every shred of his clothing. His arms and hands were in constant motion, his hands grasping in his semi-consciousness, the air or any object they happened to come in contact with. He held with a firm grip in one of his gory hands quite a large piece of plug tobacco as gory as the hand that held to it. As the writer and his Hawkeye friend approached to his side, he gazed intently at them for a time his arms in motion still, and then said: "O man; won't you turn me over?"

The Iowan said in replying to this pitiful appeal; "We would be glad to help you, [but you] are now in a better position than any change would place you." He had been placed as near as could be ascertained without a closer inspection than it was possible for them to make, so as to favor his wounds, and any change, in their opinion, would have only added to his suffering. They then went away from him a few steps to view several dead bodies—confederates—lying in a heap, and then returned to the wounded man, who repeated his request to be turned over, and was again answered, as before, in a kindly tone and spirit. "Well, if you won't turn me I'll turn myself, it don't make any difference anyway, I am dying," and making an effort with his arms and one leg that had hitherto been motionless, he turned himself upon his right side in which position they left him, just as the curtains of night were dropping to shut out the light from the gory field of death and suffering. The next morning—Sunday—bright and early the writer visited the field of the late conflict again, turning his feet at once to the tree where the poor wounded confederate had been left for his condition and pathetic appeals had disturbed, the night's slumber and dreams of the writer. But he found upon arrival that the "death angel" had preceded him, many hours, and relieved the spirit of the unfortunate enemy from its suffering environments, and it is hoped conveyed it to fairer fields where wars come not.

Now the query, all along these years has been ringing in the ears of the writer, "Should he have yielded to the dying request of the fallen foe, and assisted him in turning over, notwithstanding the fact that he believed the act would hasten his death," and his conscience has not as yet settled the matter. However he is glad to say that his failure to do so, was not because the poor fellow was his enemy, which is some consolation any way. Our own wounded in the battle were first removed and cared for, then the enemy's were looked after, and so with the burying of the dead. The confederate dead however were buried by the colored men, who had come into our lines, and it was quite amusing and yet it savored far too much of heartlessness to enjoy a laugh at the performance. The trenches having been prepared, the "contrabands" of color would take an ordinary army blanket—four "darkies" to each blanket—and lay it down by a dead Johnny, roll him into the center of it, then with one on each corner of the blanket they would "tote" as they called it, the dead to the common grave or trench, and with apparent pleasure, dump the remains into the pit, repeating as they did so, "close up gray backs," [96] and as they went for another body they would sing "Massa Linkern am a cummin," or make a song for the occasion. Looking back upon those bloody days we wonder how such things could have been tolerated. But war makes a callous conscience, you know, which is another reason why differences between nations, sections and classes should always be settled, without appeal to arms. If any class of persons, anywhere, or ever, could be justified in such acts as has just been related, it would most assuredly be the class of persons, who were the actors in this drama—the ex-slaves of our beautiful Southland—whose backs had often "smarted" from the lash of the master and driver.

> Think ye masters iron hearted
> Lolling at your jovial boards;
> Think how many backs have smarted
> For the sweet your cane affords." [97]

These lines taken from an old school book, in use in ante-bellum times (in the north only) are expressive of slave times, and no doubt aided many in moulding their minds against the "peculiar institution."

Yes, the darkies loved to see the confederates "close up."

[February 6, 1903]

The night of the second [first] day of the battle of Corinth, Oct. 3, 1862, the writer slept with a citizen clerk in the commissary department, in an upper room in the commissary building. This building, when Corinth was in possession of the confederates, was furnished with nice convenient bunks which remained intact. One of these—a good wide one—the writer and his Hawkeye friend had "fixed up" in ample shape with all the requisites of a real bed, except the feathers, if indeed they are an essential to such a luxury, and he can say that he slept well, too, until the nasty rebels aroused him from his slumbers, just before daylight by throwing a few shells uncomfortably near to where he was so comfortably snoozing, after an arduous day's labor drawing spirits from whiskey barrels for the use of the officers and men, on the bloody field, a mention of which he has heretofore made.

During the night wagons were constantly coming in and were corralled on the public square, a large fire being kept up to aid this work. The light from this fire also aided the enemy in getting a pretty accurate range on the town, especially that part of it covered by the commissary building in which the writer was peacefully reposing until the boom of the guns awoke him so unceremoniously.

The first shot, or rather shell, was fired as has been indicated, just a little before the break of day, and the report of it rang out on the breeze that still calm morning seemed to awake from its quietude and slumber all nature, within the four cardinal points of the compass, and being as it were heaven and earth together. It aroused the writer and his bed fellow in a jiffy any how. The Iowan, who occupied the foreside of their bed bounded out of bed at once, and thrust his head out of a window right at hand, just as the second shell came whizzing along on its bloody mission, exploding just before reaching our building, making a terrible racket

109

as the pieces struck against some loose boards lying in their range, which caused the Hawkeye to withdraw his head in a quicker motion than it was thrust out, saying as he did so, "This won't do me" and commenced getting into his wearing gear with the utmost alacrity, if not delight.

Hardly had the words escaped his lips when the third visitor following in the wake of its predecessors, with its "fuse" a little better timed came along, and "busted" right over the heads of the two aroused sleepers, with nothing between them and the broken pieces of the exploded shell but the sheeting and shingles, and the latter were pretty badly scattered by the fragments of the shell. This event fairly lifted the writer out of his bunk. Anyway he sprang up and out, and repeated, instinctively, the words uttered by his sleeping mate moments before, "this don't suit me either," and got inside his navy blue pants and coat in such haste, as to be ready to go below with his mate who had a few moments the start of him in the matter of dressing. The stairway was on the outside of the building, and next to this side were heaped up hundreds of barrels of pork, in a pyramidal shape, nearly as high as the building itself. As they were descending the stairs, a shell dropped among these barrels with an ominous thud, that fairly lifted the hats from their heads but the fuse was defective, and no explosion followed, otherwise destruction and death no doubt would have been the result, for upon the platform at the foot of the stairway and in front of the building quite a number of citizens and soldiers had gathered, all of whom the writer and his mate as well would have been exposed to the ravages of the explosion. A bad fuse is a good thing sometimes; upon reaching the platform the writer went to the corner of the building and leaning against it, watched the movements of the crowd of citizens and soldiers, whom the morning "shelling" had excited to fever heat, and caused them to congregate in front of the building, with a view to protection presumably, and he soon discovered that the crowd was constantly increasing in numbers and excitement.

[February 13, 1903]

He had occupied his station but a few moments at the corner when the Johnnies, who had been sending their pestiferous shells into other parts of the town, and had thereby given the commissary building a few minutes rest, now turned to their "first love" again, and sent a real live old time percussion shell, that came swishing whizzing and screaming along, and passed so uncomfortably near the head of the writer, that he absolutely "ducked" that member of his body in order to give it a free pass to its journey's end, whatever that might be. It was the closest call "to kingdom come" that he ever knew himself to get, while wearing the "blue." He is certain he felt the air that its flight put in motion fan his cheek as it passed over his head. It struck the ground and exploded in the center of the public square, where the dust was at least three inches deep, and the writer is here and now prepared to assert forty years after the event, without a thought or any intent whatever to exaggerate, that the force of the explosion of that shell hurled the dust at least fifty feet high, and to the four points of the compass in proportion, and was so thick and dense that the sun's rays did not penetrate it for some minutes after the occurrence. Old Sol had just arisen, and the cloud of dust was between him and the writer, so he is not guessing at the facts so far at least as they relate to this part of the incident.

He will readily concede that some of these old gray bearded, ex-soldiers, when in the story telling humor, can and do shame—almost—the truth, in telling a "tender foot" their army experiences. But his story, the writer dares to claim is "straight goods," unless the near approach of the said shell to his "cranium" had so warped his perspective faculties and distorted his vision, or in other words had so "scared" him that he could not see straight. A condition, which if charged, he would most certainly deny with just indignation, in fact he would be tempted to deny it, if it were even true.

As has before been stated, quite a considerable number of men had drifted to and remained in front of the building used as a commissary. Many of these were stragglers from the army. About nine o'clock in the morning, when the battle was raging fiercest, a lieutenant, who was doubtless an aid to some officer of rank, came riding by this gang, stopped and seeing so many soldiers in it, he said to them, with more cuss words thrown in than were really necessary to convey his meaning, and more than the writer will repeat after him, "what in -----are you doing here you -----cowardly hounds fall in and march to your regiments or I'll arrest every ---- one of you, for cowardice," and they did "fall in" too, and were marched by the Lieut. on the "double quick" toward the battle field, some of them without arms too. Whether or not they were given a chance to "smell burned powder" on the bloody field the writer never knew. He hopes they did, for the honor of the American soldiery, and that they redeemed themselves e'er the day was won from the enemy, like the 17th Iowa Infy. did.

It will be remembered by those who have followed the writer in these reminiscent articles, that this regiment "showed the white feather" [98] at the battle of Iuka, which was fought some two weeks before the battle at Corinth, and that "Old Rosey" in his order congratulating the men engaged in the fight on their splendid victory, excepted the Hawkeye regiment and expressed the hope that it would embrace the first opportunity given and redeem itself. The battle of Corinth presented the opportunity, and well did the regiment improve it, as the dead in its front amply attested. It was said that the enemy in front of Hamilton's division in which was the 17th Iowa, displayed extraordinary courage, marching into the very jaws of death, with unfaltering step and ranks broken only by the balls of the blue coats, by which they were fairly annihilated, the Iowa boys excelling in the annihilating business, and so removed the stain from their record, a reminder that, "He that fights and runs today, may live to fight another day," and not run.

The 12th Ill, Vol. Infy. of which regiment George White,[99] James Morrow [100] and the late T. H. Sidenstricker, of this city were members, arrived at Corinth in the evening preceding the first days battle. As the writer was acquainted with some of the boys in Co. E, from Edgar county, of this regiment, he in company with "Uncle Jimmy" Laughhead,[101] member of the 7th Ill. Cav. well known to the older citizens of Newman, who had two sons-in-law, James Morrow and John Stout,[102] in this company, called upon the boys immediately after its arrival, and learning that it was ordered into battle early in the morning they were on hands to see the boys go into the fight. The regiment at this time was in command of Colonel Chetlain,[103] a brave officer, and afterwards promoted to a Brigadier General, and he commanded a body of brave men too. The regiment bivouaced during the night at the east side of the town and just south of the Memphis and Charleston R. R. without putting up their tents. Quite early in the morning the regiment formed in line, preparatory to its march for the field of strife but a short distance to the west, from which already came in ominous sounds the rattle of musketry and the shouts of the combatants. Soon the order to march sounded and the field band struck up some patriotic air, and the brave boys caught the "time and step" at once, and tramp, tramp, tramp, as steadily as if going on "dress parade," instead of going into the jaws of death, they took up the line of march, "heads erect" and "eyes to the front." No grander sight ever presented itself to the eye of a soldier and patriot. They were on a road leading up to and past the seminary, which stood a short distance to the south west of the town close to which the battle was then raging.

The writer stood and watched the boys until they descended into a slight depression, crossed a ravine and ascended the seminary hill, their arms at a "right shoulder shift" and gleaming in the early morning sun, like stars in a cloudless sky and a clear firmament, and then passed beyond the eye's range and were in the strife for glory and victory, both of which came to them and their comrades in arms, e'er the sun veiled his face, from the gory sight, behind the western slope, the following day. It was the first and only time the writer ever had the opportunity of witnessing a body of soldiers march deliberately into the field when the battle was already raging, and the order and courage displayed by them, raised a query in his mind, that still at times, disturbs his thoughts and causes him to don his thinking cap. The query was and is "What is the nature of the force or sentiment behind or in the man that enables him with apparent ease, to march into the very 'jaws of death.'"

We can conceive how a man in anger or under excitement may brave death without flinching or tremor. But men do not go into battle usually under such conditions. Certainly the boys or men just alluded to above did not. What steeled them for the discharge of this supreme duty of a soldier? Was it animal or moral courage purely? or was it a combination of the two? or did one of these sentiments effect one man and the other another one? Would the answers of the battle scarred veterans be uniform? Ask them. The writer answering from his meager experience, would say, as he heard a brave unflinching comrade from the ranks, once say that he "could not afford to do otherwise," by which he means that from a moral standpoint he could not afford to sacrifice his self respect and manhood and face the consequences among his fellows.

[February 20, 1903]

CHAPTER SIX

AFTER THE BATTLES

The Search for a Fallen Friend

The writer has been "scared" more than once, but was only once fully "frightened." And he will undertake to explain where and how it occurred. In August, 1862, Eli Hopkins, a comrade of the writer and, by the way, a brother of our Samuel Hopkins, and Mrs. Scott Burgett, of this city, died in the hospital at Iuka, Miss., and was buried there. His father, the late James Hopkins, was very anxious to have the remains of his son brought home for final burial among his loved ones in the old home cemetery. At the request of Mr. Hopkins, the writer made an effort to carry out his desire. At the time the effort was made, Nov. 1862, by some sort of an arrangement between the Federal and Confederate authorities, Iuka was in some degree neutral grounds. That is as the writer understood it, the Confederate wounded at the battle of Corinth which ended Oct. 4th, 1862, and fell into the hands of the Federals and were by them turned over to the charge and care of the Confederates, Uncle Sam furnishing the rations and medical supplies only. Iuka was the place selected for the hospital and was, as noted above, to be considered as neutral territory, into which either side could enter only under a flag of truce. So it may be seen that the writer could get into Iuka at this time only with a flag of truce.

Fortunately, Col. Henry V. Sellers, [104] of Paris, Ill., now one of the circuit judges of his judicial district, was the provost marshal at Corinth. He therefore went to the provost to consult him about getting down to Iuka. He had never met the Colonel before, but was favorably impressed with him at first sight. The result of the interview was that he could go the next day with the Colonel, who was going by rail to Iuka with supplies. But he would not be allowed to take anything with the semblance of written or printed matter, or of a defensive nature whatever.

About one o'clock p.m. the next day train started, having no one on board but the Colonel, the writer and the train crew, the white flag floating from the front of the engine. The progress was slow and we did not arrive at Iuka until about three o'clock. A Confederate officer and a few citizens were at the depot when the train pulled in. The officer and Col. Sellers went arm in arm to the headquarters, followed by a citizen of Mobile, Alabama, who was there on the same mission as the writer, and went with the writer, but not with locked arms, however. The Mobilean had with him a copy of a daily paper published in his city which he gave the writer.

This paper was a curiosity in material and make up. The material was of the cheapest kind of wall paper and was printed on one side of the paper only, and was about 12 by 15 inches in size and was largely filled with local business advertisements, there being very little local or war news in it. One merchant, he remembers very distinctly, called the attention of the public to the fact that he still had on hands a limited amount of choice tea, that he had received from the last vessel that had run the blockade, which he was selling at

$16.50 per pound. This would look somewhat "fishy" if it was not remembered that the circulating medium in Mobile was Confederate "script" [scrip] at this time, which was as bad as Mexican dollars or as "16 to 1" would be now.[105]

The writer went to the headquarters, which occupied a part of the Iuka Springs hotel, a magnificent building erected for the accommodation of persons who resorted to the springs located there, which possessed medicinal properties of a high order, it was claimed, and consulted the commandant holding the rank of Colonel in the C. S. A. about a pass out to the cemetery located a mile to the east of the village. He appeared to be a genial, accommodating man, and he informed the writer that he would require no pass to get to the cemetery and that he would not be molested by any one. So with this assurance of safety the writer started "a foot and alone" [106] for the city of the dead. It was about 3:30 p.m. a gloomy, misty afternoon indeed. But he knew the way, in fact had been there before, when the Yanks were in the saddle. The road after ascending an easy slope from the spring branch winding around the eastern extremity of the town entered a most beautiful grove of native trees, their foliage being in its "brown and yellow sear." The road was also level and ran direct to the cemetery. The writer walked at a brisk pace and when nearing the place he, casting his eyes ahead, discovered a man coming toward him, who upon closer inspection proved to be a regular Confederate soldier in the dress of a private and was fully armed. That this discovery scared the writer all over and through him is putting it much less than the real truth. He was, in fact, frightened out of his very boots. He was unarmed, was meeting an enemy in arms, it was a dark and gloomy evening in a dense woods and was entirely at the mercy of a man with whom he was at war. All of which flashed upon him in an instant. What could he do? To run would have been useless, because it would have shown guilt, if not fear as well, and it would have also invited a chase, if not a shot from his old musket, and perhaps both. Frightened as he was, the writer, at this late date is here to say that his thoughts came quickly, thick and fast and a conclusion reached before the blue and gray met face to face, which was within less than two minutes after the "reb" was first sighted. The writer never slackened his pace, but let his feet run, figuratively, with his thoughts until the collision came, which he is pleased to say, was a harmless one. The writer said, "Good evening," and the Johnny repeated the words and added thereto "sir." And both stopped, then the writer said, "It is, indeed." Then "It's a gloomy evening?" and the "gray coat" replied, "It is indeed." Then they "eyed" each other for a moment or two and said nothing, then the writer said, pointing in the direction of the cemetery, the fence enclosing which being painted white was plainly visible, "is that the cemetery?" And he—the writer—knew as well as did the Reb that it was, but you see he did not think of anything else to say, and the representative of the Southern Confederacy answered, "It is, sir, but I guess you are too late." The answer staggered the unarmed Yank for the moment as it seemed to be complicating matters. But he was in for it and there was no retreat in sight, so he ventured to say, "Too late for what?" And smiling at the writer's confusion, no doubt, the Johnny reiterated the last part of his answer. And dropping his head for a moment he added, "Oh, well, go on, you may be in time," and shouldering his arms, which had been brought to "an order arms," and left the trembling Yank in his confusion and doubt, which to this day has never been solved. But he has settled down to the conclusion that the Johnny had been at the home of the sexton which was within the cemetery enclosure and that he had heard the family speak of some one that was to call on them for tea, perhaps, and it was then after the appointed hour, and he supposed the Yank was the delayed party who had missed a good dinner. If the reader will agree not to attribute the fact that the writer, on this occasion, was "dressed up" to his variety, nor as a reason why he supposed the Confederate soldier had taken him for the sexton's invited guest, he will mention here the important parts of his dress, the external ones, anyhow, viz: a jaunty McClellan cap, [107] an officer's coat without shoulder straps or other insignia of rank upon it, a vest to match, a black pair of cavalry pants, doubleseated, and—and—for the life of him he can't say whether his feet were covered with boots or shoes, nor does it matter in the least, for if he had have been in his bare feet his "wearing gear" even then would have so eclipsed the Johnny's" "duds" that he would have been excusable for believing the Yank was fixed up for company. But he wasn't. Uncle Sam was a better provider than the rebel government was, that was all.

The writer hastened to the cemetery and after a diligent search he failed to find among the silent sleepers the grave of his fallen comrade and neighbor. He learned long after this time that an army grave yard had been made nearer to town, for the sake of convenience, and it is quite probable that young Hopkins, who gave his life for his country, was laid to rest in this new cemetery, where it will no doubt remain until the graves shall give up their dead and time shall be no more. [108]

Our train returned to Corinth that evening in safety.

[February 27, 1903]

Shipwreck on the Return to Illinois

A few days after the battle of Corinth, it became, it seemed a military necessity to send quite a large consignment of convalescent soldiers in the hospitals in and around Corinth, to hospitals at the north, to make room for the wounded in the late battle. Among this number were the writer and his friend James Laughead, heretofore mentioned in these letters. The consignment was put on board of the cars on the Mobile and Ohio railroad, and carried to Columbus, Ky, the then northern terminus of the road, some 20 miles below Cairo on the Mississippi river. Here they were transferred to a steamer and ordered to St. Louis. But upon its arrival at Cairo it was ascertained that the hospitals at St. Louis were then over crowded with patients. So the boat was ordered to take its human freightage to the Marine hospitals [109] at Mound City [110] some eight or ten miles above Cairo on the Illinois side of the beautiful Ohio. Our boat left its mooring at Cairo just about sunset for Mound City. The day had been cloudy, and in the evening it became misty, while a brisk and somewhat chilly wind was sweeping down the river, and as the steamer was a light draught concern, without ballast, it was more or less at the mercy of the wind, and her progress against the wind and the strong current of the river, was necessarily slow. Her cargo of living freight, being convalescents, from hospitals and had to keep "housed up" in the cabins or staterooms, the weather being too inclement to permit them outside. And as it was understood that they were to remain on the boat during the night many of them were preparing for an early rest and sleep, among whom was the writer. He had stepped out onto the forecastle for a moment and had noticed the lights dimly shining through the night's gloom, of a steamer coming down the river, and had just returned into the cabin and was in the act of taking off his boots, when he heard quite a commotion in the lower deck, the jingling of bells and the exchange of signals and then there came a crash, that shook our boat from "stem to stern" knocking over chairs, tables, dishes and every "blue coat" that was not already down, including the writer and the chair upon which he was sitting. The shock had occurred so suddenly, that no one outside of some of the officers of the boat knew what had caused it. The fact was our boat had struck the steamer coming down the river, just in front of her wheels crushing in her side and making a hole deep and wide, our boat at once reversing her engine pulled loose from the other vessel which was pointed toward the Illinois shore, and as her paddles and machinery were not injured, she reached the shore before sinking, and fortunately all the crew and passengers were saved.

The collision came so suddenly and unexpectedly and was over so quickly, lasting it now seems to the writer, not exceeding five minutes, that the people, on his vessel at least, did not have time to get excited. So there was but slight confusion and no screaming, the passengers, being all soldiers, had been taught in the school of danger and were not therefore beside themselves in a scrap [scrape?] like this.

The damaged and sunken boat had belonged to the confederates and used as a gunboat by them, and was captured by the Yanks some time previous to the event and transformed into a sort of pleasure boat, and was on this unfortunate evening loaded with an excursion party consisting of about 150 persons, mostly children, from Mound City, who were going to Cairo to spend the evening, when it was run into as above described and its precious load of "sweet innocents" so narrowly escaped a watery grave. Just how the accident was brought about rumors differed. The most probable one was to the effect that in the exchange of signals a mistake occurred. It is a custom, perhaps a law, that a steamer going up stream, or against the current, meeting one running with the current has the right to select which side it shall take—right or left—and this selection is indicated by a given signal, well understood by river men. Apparently the two boats were "headed" so their prows would have clasped, at the time the close proximity to each other was discovered by the descending boat, which immediately made an attempt to prevent a collision by turning to the right, or the Illinois side of the river, but it was too late and she was struck midsides as noted above.

"Absent Without Leave"

The next morning after the accident, which occurred less than a mile below the village of Mound City, the writer visited the ill fated boat, which sunk in very deep water shortly after striking the shore. It stood in an almost perpendicular position resting on it's stern, and only a small part of it above the water. Considering the darkness of the night, and the fact that its passengers were mostly children, it seems a miracle that all escaped. The boat containing the hospital outfit landed at the wharf of the little village of Mound City at about 8 p.m. the boys remaining on board until morning. The morning was cold and chilly with a heavy mist falling, nevertheless the convalescents were formed in line, after leaving the boat, and marched to the hospital—so called—which was some half mile below the landing, each carrying his outfit of clothing and keepsakes. Arriving at the loud sounding name of "Marine hospital," which had been a hog slaughter house, but then transformed—in name only—into a human slaughter pen, they were kept standing outside, in the inclement weather, made more disagreeable by the dense fog arising from the river upon the banks on which the "pen" stood, until their names were registered and remembered, and each assigned to a cot numbered the same as his register number. This over, the "convalescent" deposited his "traps" under his cot, and he was given the freedom of the "pen" and all inside the guard limes.

The building had been designed for, and erected and used for a time as a slaughter house, the siding being put on barn fashion, and the planks not even battened, and there was no heating arrangements of any kind, in the main room used for sitting and sleeping purposes. In fact it was as before designated herein a veritable military slaughter house. The hospital—so called [111]—was in charge of one who signed his name E. C. Franklin, Surgeon U. S. A. a position he had not one qualification to fill, and it is a pleasure to the writer, to know that he played a part in ridding the service of his presence, and relegating him to the shades of oblivion, where he justly belonged. But more of him anon.

The writer and "Uncle Jimmy" stood the hospital rations and cots, one day and night and were then fully satisfied to quit and at once conspired to "slip guards" and get out of there. And they did, and in broad day light too, and went up to the village and took board and lodgings at an old time "tavern" with a "barroom without a bar," and found it a wonderful improvement upon the Marine hospital fare, and surroundings. Mr. Laughead (Uncle Jimmy) and the writer had been examined by the proper medical officer, before leaving Corinth, and had been found unfit for military service by reason of "Disability" and they were only awaiting the receipt of their discharge papers so they could return to their homes. But during the time these papers were running the "red tape" journey, which would take an indefinite time, they were under the military "Thumb" of Uncle Sam, and having left without his order or consent, the place he had assigned them—the Marine hospital—they were treading on the border—if not within the line—of desertion. The writer mentions this matter, not in a serious vein, however, but more as a prelude, or introduction to what here follows for "absent without leave" is not necessarily desertion.

There was, so far as the writer now remembers, "no roll call" of the inmates of the hospital. But as every inmate had a cot assigned him, numbered to correspond with the number on the register, an empty cot therefore, at bed time, denoted an absent inmate. And it was this fact that betrayed the absence of Uncle Jimmy and the writer. But as they had been an inmate so short a time, less than 24 hours, that no acquaintances had been formed, and they would consequently run no great risk of recognition, from name, dress or features, by anyone connected with the hospital should he run up against them; so they felt in a good degree safe from detection at the tavern. But their "sins found them out," [112] and they got their "walking papers." Soon thereafter without any marked evidence of sorrow and regret, on the part of E. C. Franklin, Surgeon U. S. A., at their parting. It is more than probable that he had come so much accustomed to parting with his patients that his treatment had sent "cross lots" to their final home that the parting with a couple of blue coats were a matter of small importance to him. The sequel of this incident will follow.

[March 6, 1903]

At the close of his last article, it will be remembered by the readers, the writer was "bo'rdn" at a tavern, having escaped from the U.S.A. Marine hospital ? [in the original] at Mound City, whither he had been sent by military authorities, by "slipping the guards," and was therefore in a certain sense in the attitude of a semi-deserter. But he now wants to say, after a reflection over the matter for more than forty years, that if this was his true attitude to his government, he would much rather bear the odium that would attach to it, than to have endured the treatment meted out to the inmates of the hospital, even for the short time he would have been detained there. The writer never had any personal experience with military-—or any other kind for that matter—of hospitals, except his 24 hours experience with the one now in question. And yet he feels impressed to say that he does not believe the U.S.A. Marine hospital at Mound City, Ill., in Oct., 1862, was a representative military one by any reason, either in make up of the building or in management. Bad and incompetent men sometimes get into places of trust and responsibility, and do incalculable harm, before they are discovered and disarmed of the power to do evil, so it was with this one no doubt, the government was not at fault. It did everything it could, and as soon as it could for the welfare of its brave defenders, whether in the field or in the hospital, adjusting all wrongs as soon as they were discovered and reached.

Long may her flag, "Old Glory," "Wave o'er the land of the free and the home of the brave." But to return to "their tale of woe," after this digression, by briefly noticing how the writer and his companion Uncle Jimmy, were discovered and "hauled over" the military "coals" by E. C. Franklin, surgeon U.S.A. and the after results. It seems that the surgeon was in the habit of meeting some of his boon companions---"hail fellow well met," at the tavern and spending the evenings or rather the nights—the first half anyhow—in games not recommended by the rules of strict morality, and imbibing drinks that bite like a serpent and sting like an adder, [113] in the end. Well, a few nights after the two deserters from the U.S. Marine hospital, had taken board and lodgings in the Mound City tavern, while the surgeon, landlord and others of the "set" were turning "Jack," sipping sod corn juice and telling tales not proper to repeat before our mothers and sisters in the parlor or kitchen, the landlord, incidentally, and without purpose, happened to mention the fact there were two "blue coats," there as guests in his hostelry. This information led the surgeon to remark, in the only way a man with a thick tongue and clouded brain could do, that is maudlin, that there were two such missing from the Marine hospital, but he did [not] know them by sight or name; but he continued, "You" referring to the host, "tell them to call at my office at 8 o'clock in the morning, promptly or they will have a ----- bad job on their hands." Immediately after breakfast the next morning the landlord delivered his message to them, at the same time indicating that they had better heed it, showing that he did not care to get out of alignment with the military authorities.

This message, emphasized by the added suggestion of the landlord, decided the two recalcitrants, to "face the music" and "beard the surgeon in his lair," [114] at the very hour he had named too. So having settled with their tavern host for their board and lodging, they started in ample time to reach the office of E. C. Franklin surgeon U.S. army and controller of the Marine hospital at Mound City, Ill., U. S. America, by the time appointed. They found the Dr. in his office, seated at a table, with pen in hand, and ink and stationery before him. Upon their entrance he turned his face toward them and said, "What will you have?" The writer replied, "That is for you to say. We understand you wish us to call at your office this morning." Dropping his head for a moment as if to collect his thoughts, and then raised it and looking them in the face, said, "O, you are the fellows who have been stopping down at the tavern are you?" "We are the chaps, sir," was the reply. "Very well," said he, "soldiers who are able to board at hotels, are able to go to their regiments, and I'll send you there." "All right," retorted the writer, "It certainly will be no punishment to be sent from a place like this to my regiment." This reply seemed to awake all the "old Adam" there was in him, [115] in a twinkling, and there was little of the "new Adam" in him. Or, if there was, it had never got out of him, and reaching up to a pigeon hole in the desk before him, he drew out a blank, which he proceeded at once to fill out, sign and hand to the writer, saying "Take the first boat to Cairo, and there you will get your transportation to your regiment."

The document which he filled out and gave to the writer, and which he still has in his possession, reads, omitting the writer's name, as follows: "U. S. General Hospital, Mound City, Ill., Oct.. 16, 1862, _____ of Co. H, 25th Rgt. Ill. Vols. is this day discharged from hospital, cured, and will report forthwith to his company commander for duty. E. C. Franklin, Surgeon U. S. A."

Uncle Jimmy, who was a much older man than the writer, being then about 55 years old, was suffered to remain in hospital, or rather remained there to suffer in it, and this would have been, no doubt, also the fate of the writer, had he have been a little less "outspoken," as to the character of the hospital. Some people do not, you know, like to have the truth about them spoken, or made public. They are like some persons, less than a thousand miles from Newman; they only "want to be let alone" [116] in their misdoings. At the time the writer was so unceremoniously "kicked," as it were, out of the hospital and ordered to report to his Co. commander for duty, his regiment was in Kentucky and as he was soon to be discharged from the service, he had no intention of rejoining his regiment, the order of Dr.

Franklin to the contrary notwithstanding. But he did take the first steamer that came down the river and went to Cairo. There he got transportation to Corinth, Miss., in the exact opposite direction from the location of his regiment, and the irate surgeon's certificate of discharge, made it possible for him to secure such transportation too. So the Dr. did for the writer just what he did not have the least desire or expectation of doing. The steamer "Belle Memphis," [117] was then running between Cairo and Columbus, Ky., in connection with the trains on the Illinois Central, Cairo then being its southern terminus, and trains on the Mobile & Ohio, Columbus being the northern terminus. The writer boarded this beautiful steamer for Columbus. She could run like a racer, and was at her best, when about midway between the two cities she struck a sandbar with such force as to lift her keel well nigh out of the water, leaving one side of her quite a good deal higher than the other. This caused such excitement and confusion among the many passengers for the time, but there was no accident. The sandbars and reefs of the "father of waters," you know, are ever drifting and changing by the erratic action and changing of the channels and currents of this wonderful river. The spars which every steamer carried, were at once brought into requisition and after a superabundance of blustering, and no end to cuss words, which river men easily have the monopoly of, the magnificent boat was soon afloat again in her native element, and gliding swiftly down the river like a thing of life, she landed her passengers at Columbus in ample time for them to take the evening train for the sunny south. It was, however, as all trains were on this road—Mobile & Ohio, at this time a military one. The writer took passage on it, and arrived at Corinth that night. Called at the general hospital next morning and transacted the business that took him there, not forgetting his friend, the surgeon of the Marine hospital at Mound City whose record, already in bad odor there, was not improved by any remarks or deeds of the writer, and he is not sorry to say that before the moon had waned and would again, the official head of the Dr. was in a military waste basket, and his other head was in search of another job. Verily "the way of the transgressor is hard"[118] --sometimes. The writer returned to Mound City found Uncle Jimmy and his "discharge papers," which had come in during his absence, and he returned home and resumed the duties of civil life again.

[March 13, 1903]

ENDNOTES

1   In 1902 the editor was his son-in-law, Moses S. Smith, who had married Isabel Root, May 20, 1893.

2   The 1860 Federal Census of Carroll Township, Vermilion County, showed J. S. McClellan as a 37-year old physician, a native of Ohio.

3   Sons of Samuel L. and Hallie Bell Hopkins. John William Hopkins, Co. H died at St. Louis, December 31, 1861. Eli Thomas Hopkins died in August of 1862 near Iuka, Mississippi.

4   The 1860 Federal Census of Illinois showed James H. (Jerry) Ishum to be 20 years of age. He was a private in Co. H of the 25th Illinois Volunteer Infantry, and was promoted to Hospital Steward.

5   Brushy Fork passes through Newman and Sargent townships, in eastern Douglas County, and Young America and Shiloh townships in western Edgar County.

6   Exodus 3:8.

7   Exodus 16:13.

8   Perhaps John Watson of Bloomfield, Edgar County, Co. A of the 25th Regiment, who died at Little Piney River, Missouri, November 15, 1861.

9   Jeremiah 51:57.

10   Source unknown.

11   In Greek mythology, the river encircling Hades over which Charon ferried the souls of the dead.

12   James Hopkins, along with his brother Joseph, private in Co. E 79th Regiment, was one of the earliest settlers at Brushy Fork timber. He was born February 12, 1815 in Pickaway County, Ohio, married Elizabeth Ann Thomas in 1838, and moved to Sargent Township, Douglas County, in October of 1841. They had ten children.

13   William B. (Brad) Shute, born in 1817, came to Newman Township, Douglas County, in 1854, and established a tile factory. He was also a farmer and builder of churches, schools, and business houses, as well as a popular tuba player in the Newman band. At the time of his death in 1889, he was survived by his wife and young daughter.

14   Daniel Jacobs lived in Newman before the Civil War and was a first lieutenant in Company H of the 25th Regiment.

15   Proverbs 13:15.

16   An important railroad junction about four miles south of the Tennessee state line and 93 miles east of Memphis, it was a Confederate stronghold. Grant's army was advancing toward Corinth when they were surprised and nearly defeated at Shiloh. General Rosecrans wrote: "The strategic importance of Corinth, where the Mobile and Ohio crosses the Memphis and Charleston ... results from its control of the movements either way over these railways, and the fact that it is not far from Hamburg, Eastport and Pittsburg Landing on the Tennessee River, to which points good freight steamers can ascend at the lowest stages of water." Robert Underwood Johnson and Clarence Clough Buel, *Battles and Leaders of the Civil*

War, Volume II, The Struggle Intensifies (Secqucus, NJ, no date), 739-740.

[17] Probably Uriah M. Banes, of Newcom (now Fisher), Champaign County, in Co. I "who drowned near Cairo May 23, 1862." *Report of the Adjutant General of he Sate of Illinois,* Volume II (Springfield, Illinois: Philips Bros. Printing, 1900), 347.

[18] Major Thomas McKibben, after arriving in Vermilion County in 1830, lived on a farm north of Danville in Grant Township, where he operated the first steam saw mill. While here he served in the Black Hawk War, and was constable, deputy sheriff and sheriff two terms, postmaster and county board member. He was in charge of the Illinois delegation at the grand rally at Tippecanoe Battlefield when William Henry Harrison was running for president.

[19] George W. was a private, Henry H. and John sergeants, and Thomas J., a first lieutenant. George was killed in a riot in Danville October 1, 1864. Several accounts of the affray appeared in the newspapers and in county histories, but one given by an unnamed Methodist preacher who was in town for Annual Conference, has not been published. "It was the year of Lincoln's second election; a large political meeting had been held during the day. There was a company of soldiers quartered in the town. Excitement ran high; Dr Ferris, a hot-blooded Southern sympathizer, who lived in Danville, engaged in an altercation with one of the McKibben boys in a store, drawing a revolver and shooting McKibben in the chest, then fleeing to his room. A brother of McKibben rushed out, saying that his brother had been shot. A squad of soldiers followed Ferris to his room, climbed the stairway and shot him. They dragged Ferris down

the stairs, shooting into him as they came out into the street, and up the street to the Court House square where he remained most of the night, still alive. Excitement ran high, men shouted, women ran through the streets, and from the windows waved handkerchiefs and cheering the soldiers." (Archives, Illinois Great Rivers Conference, United Methodist Church, MacMurray College, Jacksonville, Illinois)

20 Bird S. Coler, a son of W. N. Coler, grew up in Urbana, and was comptroller of New York City in 1900. The elder Coler was the second lawyer to locate in Champaign County, started a bank and helped start a newspaper. He served on the defense team in the murder trial of Thomas Atterberry, with Abraham Lincoln and Leonard Swett, at Urbana, April 1, 1859, which they lost. He moved to New York in 1872.

21 Col. Wesford Taggert, son of James and Jane Wadell Taggert, was born in Brown County, Indiana, near Nashville, and migrated to Charleston in 1860. He married Miss Julia Skinner, January 20, 1859. During the Civil War he raised and served in Co. E, participating in many battles, and was mustered out in 1864. After the war he was a grocer and buggy manufacturer, sheriff, member of the city council, and was elected to the House of Representatives in 1886. He was unable to attend the 1906 reunion, and his friends noted: "The colonel has a fast hold on the love and esteem of every surviving veteran of the old l25th regiment." He died later that year.

22 Col. Richard H. Nodine was born in New York, and was past 35 years of age at the beginning of the war. A major in the 25th, he was the engineer officer on the staff of General A. D. McCook during the Battle of Stones River.

23 The chaplain's name is here spelled Mericar, but no one by that name could be found in the Adjutant General's Report. However, Philip Neville Minear, son of Dr. Solomon Minear was. Minear, 25 years of age at the time of this incident, was pastor of Indianola Methodist Episcopal Church in 1861. It was reported that he was in the midst of preaching the Sunday morning sermon when news of the firing on Fort Sumter arrived. He immediately closed the Bible and began organizing a company, which he subsequently accompanied to the front. (From a hand written note in the files of the Archives of the Illinois Great Rivers Conference, United Methodist Church) He served as chaplain from August 2, 1861, to July 11, 1862.

24 Lines L. Parker, son of John W. and Hannah Pangburn Parker, was born in Brown County, Ohio, in 1832, and migrated to Elwood Township in Vermilion County when Lines was five. He was educated in the Vermilion Grove Friends Academy, then taught school in Iowa until returning to Illinois in 1854, making his home in Dallas (Indianola). He married Mary West, April 14, 1855, and was the father of five children. After the battle of Pea Ridge he was promoted to First Lieutenant of Co. D of the 25th for meritorious services. He was mustered out in 1864 and re-enlisted as Captain of Co. E of the 150th Illinois Infantry. His brother, Samuel M. Parker, was killed at the Battle of Kennesaw Mountain, Georgia, where so many from Eastern Illinois died. Lines served as an assistant agent for the Freedmen's Bureau at Atlanta for a time before his discharge. Upon returning home he was elected sheriff of Vermilion County, then moved to Douglas County in 1868, where he was elected treasurer. A Republican, he is credited with "making" Joseph G. "Uncle Joe" Cannon, who served in the U. S.

Congress 1873-1891, 1893-1913 and 1915-1923, and was the powerful Speaker of the House from 1903 to 1911.

25   French for "Put out of combat," disabled.

26   Laurence Sterne in "Tristram Shandy" wrote: "'Our armies swore terribly in Flanders,' cried Uncle Toby, 'but nothing like this.'" Book III, Chapter 11.

27   However, Chaplain Milton L. Haney of the 55th Illinois lamented the 30 days it took to cover the 17 miles from Shiloh to Corinth. "General Halleck had one hundred thousand men and ought to have gone into Corinth and captured the rebel army in three days, but he put in a month of piling up breastworks day after day and mile after mile, and let the whole rebel army slip out of Corinth with their arms and largely with their supplies at last. We lost more by sickness and delays than we would have lost in the two or three sharp battles which we would have suffered to capture the city." Milton L. Haney, *The Story of My Life* (published by the author, 1904), 159.

28   The Illinois regiments involved in this campaign were the 42nd, 27th, 22nd, 51st, 26th and 47th..

29   Perhaps from Shakespeare's "Macbeth," Act III: "Duncan is in his grave; After life's fitful dream he sleeps well."

30   It is said during the battle "Old Abe" "flew, shrieking defiantly" at the enemy, and that the regiment followed, driving them back. Confederate General Price hated the "Yankee Buzzard" and would have preferred taking him, dead or alive, to a dozen battle flags. He survived 36 engagements, and was wounded at Corinth and Vicksburg, but his luck seemed to cover his bearers, as not one of them was wounded carrying him. He had been taken from his nest in 1861 by Chief Sky, a Chippewa Indian, who traded him to a farmer for a bushel of corn. He was eventually presented to company

C of the 8th Wisconsin Regiment, that came to be known as the "Eagle Regiment." Brought home by his regiment in 1864, he was given to the governor, then was transferred to the state. He was kept on the capitol grounds and died March 26, 1881, as a result of a fire near his cage a month earlier, aged 20 years. Exhibited at many fairs he was a great attraction at the Centennial Exposition in Philadelphia in 1876. The mounted body was consumed in another fire in the Capitol in 1904, then a replica was shown for years. "Old Abe" is on the shoulder patch of the 101st Airborne Division.

[31] Actually, Federal troops outnumbered Confederates 110,000 to 80,000.

[32] Lawrence E. Root, Company K, 3rd West Virginia Regiment. Reportedly, he was at age 14, "the youngest private soldier on record." John Cresham, *Historic and Biographical Record of Douglas County, Illinois,* (Logansport, Indiana, by the author, 1900), 216.

[33] Lyman H. Needham claimed that the 42nd Illinois was the first to enter Corinth. He says, "The 42nd's flag waved over the rebel entrenchments and above the court house when the 39th Ohio arrived." (From a letter dated June 6, 1862, in the Illinois State Historical Library, Springfield, Illinois; Thomas M. Eddy says that Col. David Stuart of the 55th Regiment was the first to "raise the Stars and Stripes over Corinth," and that Lt. Baker of Yates' Sharpshooters was the first to enter the rebel works. T. M. Eddy, *Patriotism in Illinois, A Record of the Civil and Military History of the state in the War for the Union,* Vol. I (Chicago: Clark and Company, 1866), 288.

[34] Gen. William T. Sherman is reported to have said in a graduation ceremony at Michigan Military Academy, June 19, 1879: "I am tired and sick of war. Its glory is all

moonshine. It is only those who have neither fired a shot nor heard the shrieks and groans of the wounded who cry aloud for blood, more vengeance, more desolation. War is Hell.'"

35 Marietta Holley wrote many popular works as "Josiah Allen's wife" from 1871 to 1914. Born on a farm in Adams County, New York, in 1816, she continued living there until her death in 1926. Holley wrote in the dialect, with malapropisms and misspelling characteristic of much of the humor of the late 19th century. She supported women's rights and other 19th century reform efforts.

36 John H. Watson. Company E, 91st Ohio Infantry.

37 "Mudsill" was the lowest class of servile laborers. Senator James Hammond of South Carolina asserted: "In all social systems there must be a class to do the menial duties, to perform the drudgery of life. … it constitutes the very mudsill of society." *Selections from the Letters and Speeches of the Hon. James H. Hammond, of South Carolina,* (New York: John F. Trow & Co., 1866), 317-319. This function, he said, was served in the South by slaves, in the North by wage laborers. Hammond thought slaves were much better supported than laborers in the North. Union troops were often referred to by Southerners as "Lincoln hirelings."

38 She apparently thinks "Supter" is a person, not Fort Sumter where the Civil War began in 1861.

39 Psalm 139:14.

40 Plutarch ascribes this saying to Plato in "Consolation to Appolonius"; also attributed to Pythagoras, Philo, Thales, Cleobulus, Bass, Solon, and Socrates.

41 Holley misspells "tours" as "towers."

42 Luke 8:2.

43 Eastport was the center of trade, wealth, and culture in Northeast Mississippi; as the head of navigation, much cargo was unloaded here.

44 Located in extreme Northeast Mississippi, Iuka was at the time described as a pretty village, noted for its mineral springs and fashionable resorts. One visitor reported: "Iuka contains a very large and fine hotel—now used as a hospital for our troops—and some very handsome private residences and exhibits, on the whole, more taste and refinement than any place yet seen in secessia." *Northwestern Christian Advocate,* September 10, 1862.

45 About one mile upstream from Eastport, at the base of small, rolling hills; now called Riverton.

46 Gen. Ben Butler issued an emancipation order for Missouri, that was countermanded by Lincoln because of fear of losing the support of the states of the Upper South.

47 Long, continuous imprisonment.

48 Hebrews 7:3.

49 This band was known as Roddy's Rangers. Philip Dale Roddey organized the Tishomingo Rangers in 1861, made up of Mississippians and Alabamans. They provided intelligence to the Confederate army as well as staging raids on Federal troops.

50 Among the many abolitionists in Kansas were those who favored direct action, some of them making raids into Missouri to free slaves. Others enlisted in the army and were sent to Corinth, where their lack of discipline was a burden to a succession of Union commanders.

51 Snowden Sargent's father Eli, born in Maryland, migrated to Ohio at age 21, came to Illinois in 1830 and settled at Walnut Point. He married Elizabeth Wood,

and after her death married Mrs. Elizabeth Berry. Eli died in 1834 and left his son Snowden to care for the family. Snowden was born in Pike County, Ohio, April 22, 1811, and came to Illinois in 1830. On July 1, 1830, he married Catherine Berry, the daughter of his stepmother by her first marriage. She died in 1847, and in March of the next year, he married Huldah Wilson. Snowden fathered fourteen children, several of whom died in infancy, only five were living in 1875.

52   Henry T. Jones, Tuscola, Illinois.

53   "But when to mischief mortals bend their will, How soon they find instruments of ill." Alexander Pope, "The Rape of the Lock."

54   II Timothy 4:2.

55   "There is, however, a limit at which forbearance ceases to be a virtue." Edmund Burke, *Observations on a Late Publication on the Present State of the Nation*, 1769.

56   A tartar was an irritable, violent, intractable person. To "catch a tartar" is to attack or oppose someone too strong for one; get more than one bargained for.

57   Mt. Pelee was on the island of Martinique, West Indies, that erupted May 8, 1902, after being dormant for many years, destroying the city of St. Pierre with a loss of 30,000 lives, everyone on the island except a prisoner in a dungeon.

58   The new fairgrounds at Indianapolis became Camp Morton in 1861, named for the war-time governor, Oliver Perry Morton, and was later turned into a prison for Confederate captives. Up to 5000 were held there at one time, with over 1600 deaths between 1862 and 1865. A bronze bust of Col. Richard Owen, commander of the camp, is in the rotunda of the state capitol, commissioned by former Confederate prisoners in recognition of his courtesy and kindness.

⁵⁹ Luke 10:45.

⁶⁰ This must have been John Buntain, who was 19 years of age in 1860, the oldest son of Thomas J. and Savell Buntain. He enlisted June 8, 1861, and was killed at Iuka, Mississippi, August 21, 1862. He was a member of Company F of the 21st Regiment, recruited in Edgar County. Root notes later that two men of the area around Iuka were charged with harboring the killers.

⁶¹ "See the conquering hero comes!
Sound the trumpets, beat the drums!"
These words were used in Handel's "Joshua" and "Judas Maccabaeus," the text was written by a clergyman, Dr. Thomas Morrell.

⁶² Defined as a hot-tempered person always ready to quarrel or fight, referring to Southerners who were eager for a war with the North.

⁶³ With the enactment of the Kansas-Nebraska Act in 1854, emigrants from both the North and South flocked to Kansas, hoping to secure its admission to the Union as either a free state or a slave state, with consequent armed clashes. Pro-slavery Missourians who crossed the border to vote for pro-slavery measures or to intimidate partisans were known as "Border Ruffians," and the clashes came to be known as "Border Warfare." The "free" town of Lawrence, Kansas, was sacked by pro-slavery forces and in retaliation John Brown instigated the "Pottawatomie Massacre," the murder of five pro-slavery colonists at Pottawatomie Creek. Kansas came to symbolize the excitement the struggle over the attempted extension of slavery was creating.

⁶⁴ Leviticus 25:10.

⁶⁵ Benjamin F. Ford, Tuscola, was captain of Co. H of the 25th Illinois Infantry, from November 7, 1862, to March 2, 1863.

66 Robert Burns, "To a Mouse," 1785.

67 Many Illinois men joined Missouri regiments when the Illinois quota was full. The 9th Missouri eventually became the 59th Illinois.

68 Philip Sidney Post, born in 1833 in New York State, was the son of a War of 1812 veteran. He moved to Galesburg in 1834, went to law school and began practice in Kansas. He returned to Galesburg and entered the service as Second Lieutenant of Company A of the 59th Illinois, and was promoted to Brigadier General. He was seriously wounded at Pea Ridge, Arkansas, but rejoined his regiment at Corinth, where he commanded a brigade. At the end of the war he left the army and was appointed to the foreign service, being consul at Vienna. He returned to Galesburg in 1880, where he was an eloquent public speaker and commander of the Department of Illinois of the Grand Army of the Republic.

69 Oliver Bell was born in Muskingum County, Ohio, October 4, 1842, migrated to a farm near Charleston in 1856, then to the farm of James Morrow, east of Newman in Edgar County in 1860. He married Miss Charity E. McCown while on furlough February 4, 1864. Wounded slightly at Pea Ridge, and more seriously when he was thrown from a horse at Iuka, he was discharged for disability October 29, 1862. His father, John S. Bell, served in the 79th Illinois. His grandfather, John Bell, had been in the War of 1812, and his son, Sherman Bell, was in Teddy Roosevelt's "Rough Riders" in the Spanish-American War.

70 John 4:37.

71 David W. Barnett, from Camargo (Douglas County), was a private in the 21st Illinois Infantry, who died in a POW camp January 23, 1864. George Davis Barnett,

son of James and Sally Barnett, was born December 10, 1840, east of Indianola (Vermilion County), Illinois, married Nancy, February 4, 1866, and had four children. Barnett enlisted in Co. D of the 25th Illinois Infantry as corporal and mustered out as a sergeant. He was wounded three times during the course of the war, but lived many years until his death December 8, 1923.

72 Perhaps from Donald Grant Mitchell: "Misery treads on the heels of joy, anguish rides swift after pleasure," in "Reverie of a Bachelor."

73 Charles A. Clark was born in Ohio in 1827, and was killed quelling a mutiny November 25, 1862. His wife's name was Elizabeth and they had one son.

74 This incident occurred about seven miles west of Iuka and thirteen miles southeast of Corinth.

75 The Methodist Episcopal Church, South, was formed in 1845, a year after the division of the denomination over the issue of slavery.

76 A compromiser. Charles Farrar Browne ("Artemus Ward") in "The Crisis," commented: "My politics, like my religion, being of an exceedin' accommodatin' character." A "policy order" would be the same.

77 Perhaps a misquotation of John Heywood, "To hold with the hare and run with the hound." "Proverbs," Part I, Chapter X.

78 A disreputable place where liquor was dispensed.

79 To mix up type.

80 "Thus passes away worldly glory." (An anonymous saying)

81 The 8th Wisconsin, about 300 men of the 5th Minnesota, two guns of Dees' Battery, and about 300 of the 7th Illinois Cavalry, no more than 1,100 total. *Northwestern Christian Advocate*, October 8, 1862.

82   *Battles and Leaders of the Civil War* gives Union losses as 141 killed, 613 wounded, 36 captured or missing, a total of 790. (Volume I, 738).

83   General W. S. Rosecrans, in his Official Report, noted that Hamilton's and Stanley's divisions "drove the enemy's cavalry skirmishers steadily before them until we arrived within 1½ miles of Iuka. ... Here we found their infantry and a battery, which gave our advance guard a volley. ... The action opened immediately with grape and canister from the enemy's battery directed at ours, and sharp musketry fire from his skirmishers. ... The enemy's line of infantry now moved forward on the battery, coming up on the Fifth Iowa, while a brigade showed itself on our left and attempted to cross the road toward Colonel Percezel. The battle became furious. Our battery poured in a deadly fire upon the enemy's column advancing up the road, while musketry concentrated upon it, soon killed or wounded most of our horses. When within 100 yards they received a volley from our entire line, and from that time the battle raged furiously. The enemy penetrated the battery, were repulsed; again returned, were again repulsed, and finally bore down upon it with a column of three regiments and this time carried the battery. The cannoneers were many of those bayoneted at their places. Three of the guns were spiked. ... The Fifth Iowa maintained its position on the right against a storm of fire from the rebel left and center, and even when the battery was carried its left yielded but slightly, when Boomer with a part of the Twenty-sixth Missouri came up to its support, and maintained its position to the close of the fight. About this time it was deemed prudent to order up the First Brigade of Stanley's division, which went up with a shout. ... Here the rebels made a last desperate

attempt with two Mississippi brigades, ... a volley drove them back in confusion. The Second Brigade followed, and in the dusk of evening and the smoke of battle reached the very front of the Eleventh Missouri. The roar of musketry was terrible, but Mower met the shock and stood firm. The rebels recoiled and firing ceased throughout the line. W. S. Rosecrans." Robert Scott, *War of the Rebellion; A Compilation of the Official Records of the Union and Confederate Armies;* Series I—Volume XVII, 72-75.

[84] The brigade of which it was a part lost five killed, 176 wounded, and five missing.

[85] Gov. Richard J. Oglesby had always opposed slavery and under his leadership Illinois would be the first state to ratify the 13th Amendment abolishing slavery. Along with John Hanks he carried the rails that Lincoln supposedly had cut in young manhood into the Republican Convention in Decatur in1860, creating enormous excitement, thus inaugurating the "rail splitter" legend. After being wounded and serving in non-combatant roles, he resigned in 1864 and was elected governor of Illinois.

[86] No one expected Oglesby to survive, even the medical director of the Army of the Tennessee, Dr. John Holstein, who declared his wounds mortal. Unable to find the bullet, they bandaged him and waited. Still alive at dawn, hope began to build that he might survive. President Lincoln was much concerned, telegraphing Grant to send additional doctors; Dr. Silas Trowbridge and his assistants soon arrived. Oglesby had been his patient and friend in Decatur.

[87] The Second Brigade under Oglesby lost 38 killed, 222 wounded, 73 missing, total 333. *Battles and Leaders*, Volume II, 759.

88   The source of this quotation has not been located.

89   The Confederates nearly won the battle. "In the Battle of Corinth, October 4, 1862, when twenty-seven of their cannoneers were either killed or wounded, and four guns had been captured, Sergeant Hood, with the assistance of his cannoneer, loaded and fired a double charge of canister, along in front of the captured guns into the flank of the opposing side, checking the advance until the second line of battle of the federal troops could complete its formation." *Northwestern Christian Advocate*, March 3, 1923.

90   Col. William P. Rogers, 2nd Texas, led a third charge on the Robinett the next day and was killed just as he reached the parapet; then the Confederates began retreating. Some Confederate veterans claimed that Rogers had concluded that further action was futile, and tried to surrender by tying a white cloth on a ramrod given him by a soldier. This effort, they claimed, was either ignored or not seen.

91   General Rosecrans wrote in his *Official Report*: "Early in the morning the advance, under Colonel Oliver, found strong indications that the pressure under which he had retired on the 2d came from the advancing foe, and accordingly took a strong position on the hill near the angle of the rebel breastworks with his three regiments and a section of artillery. By 9 o'clock the enemy began to press them sharply and outflank them. Brigadier-General McArthur, whom I had requested to go to the front, reported wide spread skirmishing, and said the hill was of great value to test the advancing force. I ordered him to hold it pretty firmly with that view. About 10 o'clock word came that the enemy were pressing the point hotly, and that reinforcements were required or they must yield the position. Our troops fought with

the most determined courage, firing very low. At 1 p.m. … it became evident that the enemy were in full strength and meant mischief. … It was pretty clear that we were to expect the weight of the attack to fall on our center, where hopes had been given by our falling back. Davies … was told to hold his ground obstinately, and then, when he had drawn them in strongly, Hamilton would swing in on their flank and rear and close the day. … Owing to the tremendous force with which the enemy pressed Davies back Stanley was called with his division into the batteries, and sent a brigade, under Colonel Mower, to support Davies, whose right had at last become hotly engaged. Mower came up while Davies was contesting a position near the White House, and Hamilton began to swing in on the enemy's flank … when night closed in and put an end to the operations for the day.

" … [W]hen Price's left bore down on our center in gallant style their force was so overpowering that our wearied and jaded troops yielded and fell back, scattering among the houses … Riddled and scattered, the ragged head of Price's right storming columns advanced to near the house, north side of the square, in front of General Halleck's headquarters, when it was greeted by a storm of grape from a section of Immell's battery, soon re-enforced by the Tenth Ohio, which sent them whirling back, pursued by the Fifth Minnesota, which advanced on them from their position near the depot. General Sullivan … advanced to support General Davies' center. His right rallied and retook Battery Powell, into which a few of the storming column had penetrated, while Hamilton, having played upon the rebels on his right over the open field, effectively swept by his artillery, advanced on them and they fled. The battle was over on the right.

During all this the skirmishers of the left were moving in our front. A line of battle was formed on the ridge. About twenty minutes after the attack on the right the enemy advanced in four columns on Battery Robinett, and were treated to grape and canister until within 50 yards, when the Ohio brigade arose and gave them a murderous fire of musketry, before which they reeled and fell back to the woods. They, however, gallantly reformed and advanced again to the charge led by Colonel Rogers, of the Second Texas. This time they reached the edge of the ditch, but the deadly musketry fire of the Ohio brigade again broke them, and at the word 'Charge!' the Eleventh Missouri and Twenty-seventh Ohio spring up and forward at them, chasing their broken fragments back to the woods. Thus by noon ended the battle of October 4.

The results of the battle briefly stated are: We fought the combined rebel forces of Mississippi, commanded by Van Dorn, Price, Lovell, Villeprague, Rust in person, numbering, according to their own authorities, 38,000 men. We signally defeated them with little more than half their numbers, and they fled leaving their dead and wounded on the field. W. S. Rosecrans." Scott, *Official Record,* Volume XXIX, 166-171.

[92] Confederate losses were three thousand three hundred killed, wounded or missing; fifty stands of small arms, fourteen stands of colors, two pieces of artillery and much other material.

[93] Through hand-to-hand fighting Confederate forces actually passed Rosecrans' headquarters and pushed into the city occupying the Tishomingo House and other buildings near the railroad depot.

[94] The Chicago *Tribune,* for example, reported many houses in Corinth shattered by shot and shell. One

shell plunged through the Tishomingo Hotel, killing a wounded soldier. Chicago *Tribune,* October 7, 1862.

[95] The men of Company H of the 64th Illinois were primarily from Edgar County, Capt. John H. Toner, of Paris, commander. They were known as "Yates' Sharpshooters," after Gov. Yates. The 66th Infantry, known as "Birge's Western Sharpshooters," also participated in the battle, although they were known at that time as the Fourteenth Missouri. They became the 66th Illinois on November 20, 1862. Company E was from Edgar County, Capt. Andrew E. Campbell of Paris, in command. Chaplain James M. Alexander was also from Paris.

[96] Gray backs were army lice, probably used here as a play on words relative to the Confederate gray uniforms. Even in battle the men were conscious of their unwanted passengers. In one fight a Yankee colonel was seen waving his sword with one hand while feverishly scratching himself with the other.

[97] This stanza comes from the "The Negro's Complaint," by William Cowper, written in 1795.

[98] "To show cowardice," from the notion that a white feather in the tail of a gamecock shows bad breeding and cowardice.

[99] George W. White was born in Brown County, Ohio, November 3, 1832, the son of James and Levina Drake Morrow. After two years in Montgomery County, Indiana, he moved to Champaign County, Illinois, stayed there four years, then moved four miles east of Newman (in Edgar County). He entered Co. E, 12th Illinois Volunteers, March 6, 1862, joining the regiment at Corinth, being present for the latter part of the battle. He stayed with the regiment through the Atlanta campaign, and others, concluding with

the Grand Review in Washington. He was never sick or wounded during his army service, and after the war returned to his farm near Newman. A member of the Presbyterian Church, he was a public spirited man, a generous donor to Millikin University, Decatur. In 1875 he married Miss Sarah Ann Laughead, and later Rachel Fisher. He was the father of three children.

100 Tobian Miller Sidenstricker was born in Grand View Township, Edgar County, January 27, 1841, the son of James and Rachel Falden Sidenstricker who came to the county in 1839. He married Miss Carrie Johnson in 1868, and they were the parents of four children. Enlisting as a corporal, he rose in rank to second lieutenant. Slightly wounded at Corinth, he remained in the service four years and three months, participating in the battles of Fort Donelson, Fort Henry, Shiloh, Corinth, Atlanta and the "March to the Sea." He was postmaster at Newman for many years, was on the school board, and a commander of the Grand Army of the Republic. He died April 4, 1898.

101 John, James and William Laughead were among the early settlers in Edgar County, arriving in 1838. James, born in Philadelphia, February 22, 1813, was reared in Coschocton County, Ohio, where he became a tinner and built a section of the Ohio Canal in 1830. In Edgar County he farmed and helped build a six- mile section of railroad. He married Miss Ellen Wallace, July 15, 1831, and they had six children. Ellen died May 18, 1863, and he married Minerva Lansdown, July 14, 1864, and they had two children. During his military career he served as an orderly sergeant in the 7th Illinois Volunteer Cavalry, participating in several engagements, escaping injury.

102 John Stout married Laughead's daughter Mary J.

103 Augustine Louis Chetlain, a Chicago banker, was put in charge of recruiting Negroes. David B. Geiler, a member of Co. B, 7th Illinois Infantry, wrote on December 13, 1862, to the editor of the *Evangelical Messenger* about the "Negro Coral" that was at the camp at Corinth. "There are probably from five to eight hundred, all told, of all ages, sizes, and colors. They are employed in various occupations, either as servants or in attending to their daily wants. They have now nearly completed their Winter quarters, and appear to live in peace and tranquility, which is more than some of Uncle Sam's boys can do with all the enlightenment and education they possess. The chaplain of the 12th Ill. Infantry [Joel Grant, of Lockport, from early 1861 to August 1864] oversees them, and tends to their wants both temporal and spiritual. They have divine worship every Sabbath, and I am ready to say that their minds are not so benighted that they do not know anything about the religion of Jesus. No indeed, they seem to realize their situation, and could the enemy of the negro hear their humble petitions to Almighty God for the final triumph of our arms, the restoration of peace, and the liberty of the slaves, he would modify his dislike to the sable sons and daughters of Ham." *Evangelical Messenger*, January 1, 1863.

104 Van Sellers enlisted as a private in the 12th Illinois Infantry May 1, 1861, eventually becoming a lieutenant colonel, February 19, 1864. He remained active in veterans affairs, delivering an oration at the reunion of the 64th Illinois Volunteers in September of 1889, and died April 29, 1915.

105 This was the price farmers wanted for silver in relation to gold in the late 1800s, in order to give them the ability to pay their debts after the resumption of specie

payment and the demonetization of silver in 1879 deprived greenbacks of their value for that purpose.

[106] Walt Whitman, "Song of the Open Road."

[107] A cap very similar in size to regular pattern caps, but differing in quality of material and method of construction. The McClellan types have the sides sewn to the top, rather than welted, giving them a recognizably lower appearance.

[108] Ezekiel 17:12, Revelation 21:4.

[109] This hospital was staffed by the Sisters of the Holy Cross from Notre Dame in South Bend, Indiana. A small number arrived in the fall of 1861, and more came later. Trained as teachers the nuns adjusted soon to their unfamiliar surroundings and duties.

[110] Mound City was located along the Ohio River above Cairo. At the Mound City Marine Ways three of the Eades ironclad boats were built and served as the place for repair of the western fleet. This fleet played an important part in Grant's campaign on the Tennessee and Mississippi rivers. A cemetery for the dead from the Marine Hospital was established in 1864.

[111] Root's opinion of the hospital was shared by the Bloomington *Pantagraph*, which reported on the funeral of Emanuel Keve in May of 1862: "Young Keve fell on Sunday afternoon, severely wounded, was subsequently removed to Mound City hospital, where through want of attention it is thought, he died." Bloomington *Pantagraph,* May 14, 1862.

[112] Numbers 32:23.

[113] Proverbs 23:32.

[114] Sir Walter Scott in "Lochinvar;"
"And dar'st thou, then,
To beard the lion in his den, …?" Canto VI, Stanza 14

[115] The "Old Adam," the supposed human tendency to evil/sin, or the "natural man," without Christian grace or the charity of the "New Adam," obtained through Christ.

[116] Perhaps a reference to New York's Tammany Hall, a symbol of bad government at the time.

[117] One of the best troop ships, used as General Grant's headquarters boat early in the war.

[118] Proverbs 13:15.